Sorciere

A lamentable spectacle of three women (English School, 17th century)

HORTON
RED CHILD
ETERNITY
SORCIÉRE

COMING SOON
THE EXECUTIONER
VERON
THE DOG GOD
THE WAGAHAG
DONNCHADH

Sorciere

Jess Donoho

The Sorcière

by
Jess Donoho

FIRST EDITION

ISBN: 979-8-8693-7760-9

Cover Image,
Krystian Piątek (unsplash.com)
Inset Image:
A lamentable spectacle of three women (English School, 17th century)

For more information:
JessDonoho.com

CONTENTS

CONTENTS

This book is dedicated to:

Eilish Quinn
Author of MADEA and my daughter,
who inspires me to be a better writer.

And

Benjamin Donoho
Seeker of justice and my son,
who inspires me to be a better man.

THE CURSE

I am not like you.
I do not conform to your standard.
Why should I change who I am to meet your expectation?
I am beyond your judgement.
How many times has my magic saved you or your family?
I asked nothing in return. Was kindness too much to ask?
Was appreciation not justified?
You do not know tolerance, compassion, or love.
You are self-absorbed but not self-aware.
You are afraid of what others will think,
but uncaring of who I am.
You are praying to the wrong gods.
Did you think how everything could have been better, if
only you would have just embraced me as a sister or a friend.
As a savior?
But you did not, and now it is too late.
I gave you all that I could. I gave all that I will.
From this day, I will use my gift
to get the revenge I so richly deserve.
A curse upon all.

CHILDHOOD

My people were the French speaking Acadians who lived in the boggy forests of Lac Dud Bonnet, in what is known today as Manitoba, Canada. My grandparents and their neighbors were exiled by the British during the seven-year's war in 1763. What was previously a French territory was taken by the British, who drove the French settlers out of the country.

My grandmother was a healer in Lac Du Bonnet, having been trained by the generations before her, as well as the local native tribes that populated the surrounding land. The Winnipeg, Cree, Sioux and Anishinaabe all had their own herbs and rituals for healing. Although they fought among each other fiercely, the healers shared an uncommon peace, and shared their knowledge freely. The tribes also had their spirits that were of the land and water. These spirits were called upon to bring healing to those afflicted. Although my people did not believe in spirits, they acknowledged the beliefs of each tribe, and incorporated these spirits into the healing as a show of respect. The Acadians and the tribes they encountered had traded their herbs, poultices, and tonics throughout the province.

But the wars came to this small corner of the world. In

exile, the Acadians traveled south. Although this was a dangerous time, my people forged a trail southward through the North American wilderness. The journey took them through the lands of the Odawak, Ojibwe, Ho-Chunk, Cherokee and Chickasaw. It is widely known that wherever you travel, the earth will provide everything man or beast needs for good health. Even the arid deserts provide. In this new land my grandmother found yarrow, which she applied to the skin for wounds, or to stem bleeding. It was also a mild sedative for those with anxiety. It could remove swelling caused by sprains or tears. She was introduced to the purple coneflower, which treated coughs, colds, and problems with breathing. Even the astragalus plant, which had many varieties to treat infections, relieve seasonal breathing issues from pollen and dust, even remedy heart and liver problems when used properly or mixed with other herbs. Some varieties of astragalus were fatal, and it was her task to know the difference.

As a newcomer to this land, my grandmother would trade her knowledge with local tribes and settlers as she went. She learned about the healing herbs, rituals, and the spirits of each tribe, and in turn shared her own knowledge and herbs. In this way, my grandmother was a key figure in insuring the safe passage of her Acadian community.

When the Acadians had gone as far south as land would permit, they encountered the virtually impassable swamps of the Territory of Orleans. This was lowland marsh and bog that stretched from the terra firma of the inland plains to the Gulf of Mexico. Hundreds of square miles of soupy green and brown water, much only inches, or feet deep. All of it split into tens of thousands of small bogs, marsh, and islands. At the border of the marsh, she stopped with the majority and established a village called Houma, named for the native Houmas tribe that had existed there since antiquity. Houma would grow and succeed in a hostile and remote part of the country.

It was here that my parents were born. My mother to original Acadian settlers and my father to a French Cajun family living in the deep swamp. Both were raised in the healing arts. Together, their healing arts merged into a greater vocabulary of care and welfare for the communities they served.

Later, my parents and their kin moved further south to form the village of Dulac, from the French words meaning "Of The Lake". This is a spit of dry land extending to the deepest southern land before swamps of cypress block the way to the ocean. It was wet and wild, like Lac Du Bonnet, but instead of forest, there was tropical and dense jungle. Where Acadia was a land of pristine, deep blue lakes and streams, Dulac was warm, still water, stained brown by the deterioration of leaves and the disturbance of sediments by every living creature under the surface. Acadia was a land of crisp, biting air that was dry and cold. Here in the bayou, it was hot, humid and the air was heavy. It was a swampy land, but it suited them. They were raised in a wild remote place, and in Dulac, they found the wildest and most remote land possible. Not only remote, but unwanted by others. There was little chance anyone would care to run them out of this hell on earth; but it was their hell, and they embraced it.

Settlers to these rugged places brought their native words

to describe the land. A *marsh* or *swamp* is made of large meadows, saturated with water, or large swaths of shallow waters with miles of cattail and reeds covering every inch. A marsh could be fresh water, brackish (which was a mixture of the oceans salt water and the inland freshwater), or a saltwater marsh (which was inundated with salt water). Bayou were the narrow channels of water that separated the tens thousands of small landmasses created by the buildup of sands, mosses, and algae between the roots of the cypress trees. Bogs are the soft, spongy ground and vernal pools were freshwater spring. This was country settled by the reclusive, private, and rejected of society. To live in this place was to endure the worst the world could throw at you as the price for absolute privacy and freedom.

It was here they established a trading post and a small community. While the nearest large town of Houma was only sixteen miles to the north, it could take two days to navigate the labyrinth of swamp and forest to get there. As quickly as they established a road, it would become overgrown and disappear. When the storms came, they flooded the streets and washed out the bridges and dams, still, they stayed on and claimed this small piece of land as their own.

Winters were mild, spring was beautiful, summer brought hordes of mosquitos, and the sickness they delivered. Fall was the hurricane season, bringing storms and destruction to the lowland swamps. While Acadia had giant mosquitos that swarmed, the Orleans variety were tiny, but just as voracious. Even with the storms and the bugs, we still refused to abandon what we had earned with our sweat and work.

My father traded with local native tribes of the Oumas, Tunicas and Chitimacha's. It was the healers of these tribes that taught my parent the plants, songs and prayers that healed in this part of the world. It was here that I was born in 1791. I would be raised in the wisdom of healing. As an infant I was tied to my mother's bosom as she harvested her herbs and roots. As a toddler, I sat on the table while my father pressed and pounded recipes and potions. My school was the room where they treated wounds and virus, delivered babies, and tranquilized the dying to send them off painlessly.

We were not a people of religion. To us, death, like birth, was a part of the life process. Both were a cause for celebration. The beginning and end of a journey.

†††

Our routine was predictable. Each day we would break fast, then head deep into the woods and swamp in search of the plants, roots, flowers, and fruits that we used in our healing practice.

When we returned, it was generally mother that began seeing patients while father and I prepared our harvest. We tied a hemp string to the stems of each plant bunch and hung them upside down from the ceiling. This preserved the flavors and efficacy of the medicine within. In Acadia, roots and fungus traditionally went into a cellar for the cool, dark storage, but here, with the groundwater only inches below the surface, we built above the ground floors of timber and wattle, covered in a thick mound of dirt. This insulated against the heat and humidity of the glades and allowed our roots to be preserved all season long.

Some of our medicinal plants had a very short growing season and a short effective life. These we would boil down in water, extracting the medicinal compounds, then we would preserve this extract with a small amount of distilled alcohol. It tasted foul, but it was an effective preservation. A single plant preserved was called an extract. A blend of extracts created a tincture, and a specific recipe was called a potion. Thus, we were able to build a medicine cabinet that had an effective life that transcended seasons.

As the only medical help for days around, we needed to do much with little outside assistance. For wounds, we apply a poultice of yarrow root, which stops bleeding. Plantains can have a numbing effect. Burns and mild cuts and scrapes were best treated with our wild honey. Honey is naturally antibiotic, antiseptic, antifungal and antimicrobial. While we did not understand the biology in this time, we recognized that these treatments had been used since antiquity. There are many types of anti-inflammatory plants that we can add to the honey to reduce swelling. We can make teas out of just about any plant in our native swamp with medicinal effect. The hot water steeps our medicinal compounds and when ingested, can be effective treatments for everything from cough to pain or nausea. Once our herbs are prepared, both father and I assist mother in the care of our patients.

Injuries like wounds were always easy for me. Whether a septic wound caused by infection, or a bite from one of the predators of the swamps, wounds are visible illness that can be quickly diagnosed and treated. The injuries that frightened me were the snake and insect bites. Small puncture wounds that betrayed the venom that coursed through veins and muscle. These attacks often happened at night, and the victim rarely know what kind of insect or snake had caused the injury. Some venom attacked the breathing, other the blood, or nerves. Without knowing exactly what caused the bite, we treated basic symptoms, and waited for others to appear. In cases where minutes can mean death, waiting is a luxury we cannot afford.

The other illness that confused me were the cancers. On the outside, everything looked normal, but inside, tumors or rots were occurring. The patient would lose weight and was often in great pain, but we had no method of determining if it were curable or not. If so, what to use? We generally treated the pain with hallucinogens and prayed to whatever spirits or gods came to our mind at the time. Any small advantage was taken.

Still, under the tutelage and instruction of my parents, and the visiting native healers that occasioned to travel our way, I became adept at diagnosing and treating all manner of ailment before I was ten years old.

MAKA

In my tenth year, a man was brought to my parents. His skin was as black as the onyx stone in my mother's heirloom broach. He glistened with sweat, and was in obvious pain from the large, infected wounds in his legs and wrists. Father would later tell me these were from steel manacles, or bindings, that were used in the slave trade. He had been found in the lean-to workshop of the local blacksmith, sweating of fever and delirious.

Father prepared a poultice of honey and herbe á malo also known as lizards' tail. This was a powerful healing poultice that also offered sedative properties. Mother spooned out a dose of elderberry and mangler tonic to aid in the man's chills, fever and to boost his immunity. They covered him with warm blankets and the three of us took turns watching over him through the night.

For days, he seemed to worsen. His breathing became labored, and his skin became blotchy. Father feared he would need to remove the leg, but mother persisted in her attention to the wound. In the fourth day, his fever broke, and he opened his eyes to the wood-beam ceiling of our home.

With barely a whisper, we ascertained his name was Maka, son of Makandal. Mother and father offered their names, which he repeated. He looked to me, who was cautious in the presence of this strange, dark man, and I offered my name in barely a whisper, but he had heard it and he nodded with a smile.

In the following weeks as he healed, we were to learn much from Maka. His father was Makandal, native of the Yoruba of Nigeria, and a Oungan, of the Lwa, which was an African religion that centered on the creator "Bondýe". Bondýe created spirits that could be either human or divine. The regions of Nigeria, Benin and Togo boasted millions of Yoruba people. For these tribes, Lwa was a formidable and mature religion. As an *Oungan*, or a person of integrity who was highly revered in Yoruba society, Makandal served as both spiritual and community leader.

Maka delved deep into history to share with us his coming to be on our home. The story began two hundred years prior, with the Spanish arrival in the Americas, bringing both disease and exploitation of the natives. As the Spanish conquered the Americas, they needed labor to work their lands. Men of fortune and slavers herded the Yoruba, Kongo, and Fon peoples of Africa like cattle into the holds of ships bound for Saint-Domingue, in what is today known as Haiti, the slaving capital of the Americas. Here, over five hundred thousand African men, women and children would be imprisoned next to slaves of the Inca, Aztec, and Americas. They were sold to the highest bidder as property. Some found homes that treated them as valuable investments, others were sold as tools to be used, abused, and discarded.

Saint-Domingue was a French Colonial province at the

time, brutally ruled by the Catholic Church. Under decree by King Louis XIV, Code Noir required slave owners to have their slaves baptized and instructed in Roman Catholic doctrine. This abraded many slave owners who did not want their slaves wasting valuable work time celebrating saint's days, and they feared the gathering of the religious. For slaves to come together socially encouraged talk and alliance. The slave owners feared this would lead to revolt.

For Oungan (Priests) and Manbos (Priestess') of Lwa, like Makandal, this Catholic influence, combined with the various religions of the African Nations and the South Americas became a single theology that Makandal thought had one time been a united religion that had been torn asunder by forces and geography. To put the pieces of these beliefs back together, Makandal developed an entirely new theology. One that embodied Catholicism and Freemasonry, borrowed influence from his African beliefs and those of both Inca and Aztec of the Americas, to establish a version which gutted all known religions and rebuilt them into a single belief that made sense to Makandal and his followers.

Makandal borrowed the Fon word Vôdoun, for spirit or deity, and declared this new religion Vodou. Within Vodou, Makandal became an *oungan*, his wife a *manbo*. His adherents founded small *ounfò's* (temples) for the gathering and disseminating of the Vodou religion.

Vodou was a theology of a new transcendent creator. Within this new Vodou, there were not just one Lwa, or spirit, but one thousand Lwa, each falling under the pantheons of Rada or Petwo. Rada Lwa are often seen to be of peaceful countenance and benevolence, but they can also be vindictive if displeased. The Petwo are forceful, aggressive, and dangerous, but may also be protective and generous to the living. Within Vodou, spirits could be taken into a body for both good and evil purposes. The same was seen with healing and hurting. Vodou ritual could heal the ill or be used to create injury or illness to an enemy. The ritual killing of animals was an offering to the Lwa, and the feeding gained favor and respect, increasing the power of your ritual. It was discovered that the combining of rituals from these other regions and religions amplified the strength and presence of the Lwa spirits that an oungan could use to heal, help, or harm the people.

Thus, Vodou embodied a belief that Makandal taught and practiced throughout his life in Saint-Domingue. He passed his knowledge on to his son Maka, who followed in his footsteps as a Oungan, and was highly revered by the people in his own right.

Vodou spread widely through the slave prisons within Saint-Domingue. Eventually, it spread to the Caribbean islands and Americas where it was modified into Cuban Santeria, Brazilian Candomblé and modern paganism. Over time, it would blend with the Christian religions like Mormonism. In the American South, it would become known as Voodoo, a comical and tourist version of the original religion.

As Vodou gained in popularity among the slave communities, there became a new unrest. With Saint-Dominguean slaves outnumbering Europeans eleven to one, it was only a matter of time before a revolution occurred. Makandal, along with other oungan's completed a Vodou ritual, after which they massacred whites in the local area. Emboldened, a revolution was declared, and the French sent Generals Napoleon Bonaparte and Charles LeClerc to quell the unrest. In 1801, the French conceded defeat, and Saint-Domingue became a new republic. In protest, the Roman Catholic Church abandoned Saint-Domingue, and Vodou took over the churches and congregations left behind. This transformed Vodou from a cult to a true religion.

Politics and religion are bedfellows. They rise together, but prey on each other without hesitation when challenged. Vodou had helped to liberate the Saint-Dominguean people, but with the increasing popularity of Vodou as a religion, the president of Saint-Domingue accused Makandal and many of his fellow oungan's of killing a child and eating it in a Vodou ritual. Thus, Maka's father Makandal was burned at the stake and Maka himself was put on a slave ship bound for the Americas.

The ship offloaded a portion of the slaves and trade goods in Pilottown, at the base of the Mississippi river. There, they would be transported upriver by barge. Maka and the others remaining on the ship were bound West for the Port of Houston. As they passed through the sheltered waters of Isle Dernieres, Maka had thrown himself, manacles, and all, into the water, sinking below the arrows and shot that attempted to stop him. He had held his breath underwater for long moments until his body demanded oxygen, and he erupted to the surface with the ship far beyond him. Fighting the weight of the cuffs and chains, he swam to shore. Populated only by a British outpost, Isle Dernieres, had a meager twenty inhabitants. Maka stole the small inland sailing craft used by the outpost to cross channel and island, inland to Dulac. Days later, sick and in great pain, he found the blacksmiths shop and removed his manacles. But the swamp had done its job, infecting, and festering the open wounds left behind. Had he not been discovered when he did, he would surely have succumbed to the infection.

Despite the manacle wounds, our community did not condone slavery, or the ownership of people. The community of Dulac gathered around Maka and healed his spirit, even as my parents healed his body. In return, Maka and my parents exchanged much of the healing and ritual practice of Vodou. It is said that Vodou is a magic. That it can do things that man cannot. Maka often spoke of this magic, and of the power that it contained. My parents assumed that this was the magic of healing, but Maka and I had communicated deep into the nights, he speaking, and me listening, sharing the darker and more mystical parts of Vodou that he dare not share with others. I became his student, and together we blended my knowledge of local healing with his knowledge of the spiritual world. Together we raised the gods and summoned the demons. We attempted to show my parents the magic of the spirits joining with us to heal, but they eschewed this as sorcery and false medicine. They would have none of it in their hospital, and Maka and I practiced our arts in private, deep in the swamp where no one could see.

While my parents cared for the ill in their Dulac hospital, Maka and I would travel throughout the wetlands caring for those in need. We would pack a simple parcel of foods and medicines and drift through the glades and swamps in our pirogue, a flat-bottomed boat suited for traversing shallow water. With Maka in the stern, shuttling the long wooden pole up out of the water, then planting it firmly in the mud and tea below, pushing us along the waterway, we would boat deep into the swamps searching out a rumored resident who was ill. Despite no maps or reliable description beyond a cursory direction and distance, we generally found them alive, and were able to provide healing care, or a painless passing.

It was only these remote illnesses that allowed Maka and I to practice a true Vodou. Without a formal ounfò, our efforts to bring forth the spirits were crude and unreliable. Our offerings were often too unworthy, bringing the Lwa's wrath instead of healing, but we did the best with the resources at hand. Maka would capture a small alligator or opossum during our travels and confined them to a cloth sack. Once our patient was sedated, we would stoke our fire and begin our dance, calling for an Lwa spirit. During this ritual, Maka would slit the throat of the small sacrifice, offering the life and blood to the Lwa in solemn respect. If the dance and the offering were pleasing to the Lwa, they would come into us, providing knowledge and assistance in the preparation and application of medicinal treatment. If our offerings did not please the Lwa, they would possess us and use us in the most horrific ways to show their displeasure. We learned quickly to please our Lwa.

Over time, our medicine did not resemble Vodou at all. We had taken the foundation and created something entirely new with it. Without Oungan or Manbo to guide and teach us, we experimented and played with the Lwa. Where traditional Vodou required prayer, dance, and song to all Lwa in the name of Bondýe, Maka and I each bound to single Lwa that would remain with us for our lifetimes. Our relationship was symbiotic. Not a friendship, for that would assume too much. Our Lwa were powerful beings that were entirely selfish in their actions and reactions. We offered the Lwa an opportunity to connect with the living world, and they wanted this connection. In return, they assisted us with providing healing to our communities. It was an uncomfortable partnership. Together, we were an effective team, but never did Maka and I assume a friendship or love with our Lwa.

DULAC

Dulac is a small community and will never be more. It is too remote, too hostile. It is hot and humid; the waters are filled with alligators and the air is smothered with mosquitos. In between are every manner of animal that seeks to protect itself or feed. Panthers, venomous snakes, spiders, and disease. It is all here, and only the people of the Acadia, the Creole or the desperate find home in this place. The Creole are the peoples of Portuguese, Spanish or African descent. They are the people hunted by the law and chased into the swamps where they seek to find a new life among other outcasts. All are welcome in in this place where gossip is rampant, but judgement is sparse.

As I came into my womanhood, Dulac became too small. It was from birth that I would be a healer. I was raised from infancy to this task. Dulac already had two healers in my parents. Maka had been an amazing vessel of knowledge for my parents. His instruction in Vodou and its potential to heal took my parents healing to another level. This attracted people of poor health from many miles around to our small village in the swamp. Still, my little family numbered four healers in a community of barely two hundred souls. Maka and I were not needed here.

Besides, Maka stirred an unhealthy interest in the locals. While they embraced him as a member of the community, they sensed in him a different kind of energy. Maka was borne of Vodou, and its magic. He was oungan in both spirit and leadership. Although he had made no attempt to influence or control the population, it was clear that Maka was a higher form of human. He was the leader, although none had named him so. In a community of outcasts and loners, one whose head stands tallest is often the first neck chopped off. The tension was palpable, and both Maka and I knew it was time for us to leave.

The feast provided was spectacular. Such events in Dulac are an occasion for all to celebrate, and for Maka and I to leave was cause for festivity. Yes, they loved us and would miss our participation in the community, but we were both different in ways that bred the tiniest amount of mistrust. I, in my awkward and reclusive self, and he in his spiritual aloneness. All this spark needed was a single incident to become a raging fire.

Maka and I left Dulac before the sun rose in the Eastern sky and the swamp was still and quiet. Before the bullfrogs and crickets began their morning song. Before the growling of the alligator and the cacophony of the birdsong. We had discussed this journey over the last several weeks. We determined that a small swamp settlement suited us. We would head south, deeper into the swamp, to Cocodrie. It was a mere 13 miles from Dulac as the crow flies, but it might as well have been in another country in logistical navigation. So many miles of closed and claustrophobic swamp. Poling a small flat-bottomed boat through the labyrinth of mangrove and cypress forests. There was no road, and no map. You simply continue south and ask direction at any shack you find hidden in the mangrove and moss landscape.

To a casual gaze of the swamps, it is lifeless except for the foliage and the occasional ripple on the water by a surfacing fish. Look closer and the swamp is alive. Turtles slip off into the water as we pass. The carefully camouflaged alligator sunning half-in, half-out of the water. The colorful Ibis, wood stork, herons, and roseate spoonbills, feeding along the shore. Look closer and you see whole families of raccoon foraging just out of reach of the alligators. Below the surface, the massive anhinga glide under the tea-stained surface, their silvery scales muted by the brown water, but a stark contrast when they come out of the shadows and the sunlight reflects from their long, ichthys bodies.

Cocodrie was just a few homes and small marina where swamp dwellers from deeper in the glades could come for supply and to trade their skins, furs, and fish. It was a place for those on the edge of every margin. More than outcasts or loners, those who came to Cocodrie were socially inept. They needed seclusion, privacy, and their own company more than any other. Their occasional trips into Cocodrie were like the cattlemen of the West coming into town after a long cattle drive. They were flush with cash from their trade and sought out the companionship of whores and the social comradery of the bar. They ate a beef steak in the saloon, slept on a store-bought mattress in the hotel, or on the floor of their boat (as they did hundreds of nights every year as they fished under the moonlight). They spent most of what they earned in a single night or two. They then bought meager supply with their remaining funds and pushed off from the marina in small boats to return to their shacks in the swamp.

Cocodrie is like every remote village. What you see in town is no indication of the actual population. While Cocodrie proper was a mere 34 souls, the population that it supported was nearly five hundred. My family and I had occasion to come to this place each year to assist in the healing of those who were too ill to travel. I had seen legs bitten off by alligator, those who had the poison of the water moccasin in their veins or with cancers or tumors. Both Maka and I had visited before, and we were known here. Cocodrie had been seeking a healer to live in their village, but it was simply too far away and too deep in the swamp. For Maka and I, it was the perfect choice.

We arrived in Cocodrie to a small gathering of residents and swamp dwellers who had come to greet us. Just as our departure from Dulac demanded a celebration, so did our arrival in Cocodrie. Tables were set up under the mangrove. Whole alligator turned on a spit. Its tail meat better than any chicken breast ever roasted. All manner of bird and fish was served on bark platters. A local farmer brought in ears of corn and tomatoes that were ripe and full of juice and seed. To Maka and I, he gave a gift of two red apples. Such a rare treat was this that we embraced him and his wife, a young bitter girl of less than fifteen and only a year older than me.

Her husband was twice her age, but he was a strong and good provider. She obviously did not appreciate her good fortune at having a good farmer for a husband. She was too young to understand that abusive, socially outcast swamp dwellers made a fun romp in the barn, but poor mates. She would learn, o she would not.

After the feast, we were led to a small cottage where a local ship captain had recently deceased. There were no deeds or property ownership here in the deep swamp. You made your home where you would, and the community had cleaned this small home for us to live in until we found a place better suited.

It was not likely we would ever move from this place. There was a large living area with a deep fireplace for cooking, a large dining table that would serve as both our eating area and our surgery. Fresh water was plumbed to the kitchen and into a wooden trough. A small bedroom with a mattress made of layers of wool and straw, and two layers of home-sewn quilt.

The townspeople had mistaken us for a couple. It was not uncommon for different races to marry in these places. One found companionship where one could. Females were in very short supply, and often a girl would take a husband to escape the common trade of whore, or to prevent in inevitable in-breeding that was also all too common in these remote places. As for Maka and I, we did not discourage the notion that we were a couple, but we were in no way romantically involved. Our connection was on an intellectual and spiritual level. We were singularly focused on our craft and our religion. He as the oungan, and me as the manbo. Together, we were far more powerful than apart. Our sacrifices combined, amplified our rituals, which increased our healing ability. Maka and I embodied the new Vodou of the Orleans swamps.

†††

Our practice began immediately. The community had given us their finest welcome and had relieved us of any responsibility until the festivities were over, but now there were the ill and wounded that needed immediate attention. They had patiently waited for the days it took us to arrive, and now they were desperate to be seen. Two of them had not survived the wait, there could be no more delay. Before night had fallen on that first day, a short line had been established at our front door. Maka interviewed each and created a priority based on their condition. The first three would take both of our combined attention, the others we would each see separately. We quickly unloaded our sacks of dried herbs and roots. There was no time for organization, and they are strewn about in their various jars and leather wrappings.

Before we begin, we must first bring our Lwa into our home. It is an important ritual that defines our place of worship, healing and living. Before allowing anyone inside, both Maka and I sat on the floor of our shelter. He crushed the seeds of dream root into a small cup of water, and we shared the cup. Our sacrifices were lizards and mice. Small creatures we had brought on our journey. These were humble offerings to our Lwa, but they must suffice until we could settle in and obtain more appropriate gifts. It seemed as if our Lwa understood our predicament, as they accepted our sacrifices and entered each of us, possessed and full of the benevolent spirit that guided our hands and minds through these healings. Both Maka and I shook uncontrollably as our Lwa possessed us, filling our spirit with their presence. We burned a smudge, made from the inner bark of red ucuuba trees. This would drive out any evil in the home. We were then ready to work.

Each patient was brought into our make-shift hospital and was given a tea of rhododendron and poppy leaves to induce a sedative deliriousness. This not only relaxed the patient and opened them up to the spiritual Lwa that guided us, but it also clouded their mind to the rituals and magic we used to assist in the healing. We had learned long ago that that people feared what they did not understand. Our vodou, while beneficial to these people, would likely be seen as dark magic. We must always be careful to protect our spiritual self.

While Maka crushed and blended our medicines into poultices and broths, I performed surgeries. During these healings we prayed and chanted. Often, we would stop mid-procedure to dance and sing our prayers to our Lwa. One by one, we did what we could to help and to heal. The floor of our cottage was covered in the bodies of those resting and recovering. As they arose from their induced sleep, we would assist them outside into the fresh air, where they would rest until they could walk home, or to their boats.

As the sun peaked over the mangrove, we were finishing the last of our patients. Both Maka and I were covered in blood, bile and sweat. It was painfully hot in this home, and with temperatures nearing one hundred degrees and humidity over 80 percent, we determined that the first order of business would be to modify our home to include more air movement.

Our first months were a great success. The people of the mangrove swamp learned to trust us, and we them, for we were all a naturally mistrusting species. We traded our services for food and work on our home. Ship-builders had opened an entire back of the home to open air, extending the roofline into a long veranda. A second bedroom was made for Maka, although the people believed it would be a private infirmary, and it often was. Two large windows were installed on the opposing wall to create a pass-through ventilation.

As neither Maka or I desired to eat where we treated the ill, we had a hospital fashioned as a large, covered patio, elevated three foot off the ground to keep our patients from the insects, snakes and predators that would come for them while they slept. It held six pallet-beds and featured a surgery table with running water. We had a large platter of polished brass shipped in, and this reflected our oil lamp light directly to the area we worked. The front and sides of the structure was clad in planks of mangrove that were hand split and hewn by the shipwrights. A short path led down to a small marina that accommodated four small boats for those arriving by water.

The back of the hospital was open to the air and backed up into the swamp itself. Here, protected from prying eyes and the curious, we could conduct both our vodou and our healing.

The final step was a small room inside the hospital where, in the privacy of closed doors, we built our own ounfò (temple). It was here we prepared ourselves for our daily ritual, safe from prying eyes of the village.

†††

We found community in this small marina home of ours. Each of us took care of the other in the best way we knew how. It was neither bought or bartered, it was freely given and gratefully taken. We did not think to negotiate pay prior to treatment, nor after. Several days or even weeks after a treatment, our patient would come through our doors with a sack of harvest, a brace of poultry or a basket of fresh fish. We always had more than we could use, and so we were the de facto home for the homeless or hungry. A community cauldron was set up in front of the hospital and a pottage was always cooking under a low fire. Pottage is the leavings of each meal. Whether meat or vegetable, extra food was placed in the cauldron to make a sort of stew. Day by day, as more is added or taken away, the pottage changes, never to be the same flavor twice. Frankly, it was quite delicious, and was very filling on an empty stomach. Our presence now healed and fed the body. Maka and I would talk deep into the night about whether we should also feed the spirit with knowledge of our Lwa and religion. Not today, he would say.

We showed the children of the swamps the various plants, roots, and creatures we required in our work, and they would harvest these in their travels with parents, or in small groups, for few people traveled the swamps alone. They would deliver this harvest to us fresh. The plants were stored in the rafters off our home, hanging upside down, as is the way to best preserve all medicinal plant matter. The roots were stored in a root cellar we had made above ground, for Cocodrie sat on land just inches above the waterline. There was no opportunity to store below ground here.

All through this construction we continued our work. Each day beginning with our ritual sacrifice to our Lwa. The possession by our Lwa spirits through herb and root concoctions. Our joining of spirits to increase the spiritual intensity of our magic. It felt good and right. We felt comfortable with each other, joined in our spiritual union.

Medicine was not a widely known art in these remote parts of the world. The rituals and work that most patients witnessed first-hand were entirely within the scope of what would be considered normal. We sewed up wounds, applied poultices or brewed teas. Our dance and sacrifice done to begin and end each day, out of visibility of the community. As cases came in requiring a greater healing power, we were careful to sedate our patient to insure their comfort and our safety.

As the year progressed, Maka and I delved deeper into our spiritual practice of vodou. We took increasingly strong doses of the psychedelics and deliriant's that induced our possession. We cultivated stronger and more powerful connection with the Lwa. These possessions generally lasted no more than an hour, but we took turns minding the hospital while the other would undergo possession for days. During these journeys, we would chant, dance, and sweat in the confines of our small ounfò. We would emerge from these sessions completed drained, drenched in sweat and with wild, unwashed hair and bodies. The stench of our ritual smudge, and the chemicals leaching from our bodies smelled of rotting death.

To us, these were spiritual and medical journeys that were exciting and beneficial. We became steeped in this world while outside, our close community watched and wondered. As we became more disconnected from our community, the villagers began to talk amongst themselves. While those in need always came to our hospital, those with marginal need began to stay away. No more did villagers come to our pottage cauldron, and it overflowed with neglect. No more were we greeted with smiles and confidence. Maka and I were oblivious.

One evening, the greeting from our door was not a patient, but my parents. They had made the journey south upon hearing distressing tales of our condition in Cocodrie. I pulled aside the skin that served as our door to face my mother, whose shocked look of astonishment alarmed me. I reached for her as if to comfort, and she recoiled, as if burned. She saw the puzzled and hurt look on my face and her own countenance softened. Father followed her into the house, and he glanced around the room with a veiled disgust. It was not until this moment that I realized how we had changed, not only in our personality, but in our appearance. Both Maka and I had long-since stopped caring for our personal hygiene. Our clothing had become ragged and unkempt. Our hair long and matted. Our hands and feet were caked with soil and filth. More alarming, we had become emaciated in our drug induced possession. My cheekbones stood out bony and severe, my elbows and knees were knobby and bulbous. I was nineteen years old and looked fifty.

Father looked about the cluttered and filthy home and began rifling through herbs to find the ones he sought. Mother immediately stripped off my clothes and ushered me to the lagoon to wash. Maka followed, head hung low with embarrassment and resignation.

While we bathed, mother returned to our home for essentials, and when she came back to the lagoon, she cut our hair severely short to remove the knots and gnarls. She brushed out what was left. She oiled our bodies with perfumed oils and the dressed us in our cleanest clothing.

Returning to our home, we found that father had done a passable job of cleaning, leaving whole piles of clothing and blankets outside to wash. A small crowd had gathered to watch the excitement, but we did not speak to them. We threw out bundles of mildewed herbs. We quietly cleaned out the home and then took the piles of clothes and bedding down to the lagoon to wash everything. We hung the cleaned fabric in the mangroves to dry in the heat of the day.

In contrast, our hospital was clean and presentable. We walked my parents through the building but did not allow them entry to our ounfò. Father questioned the room, and we simply steered him to the patio. He gave me a look of concern but did not press his questioning. He knew that there was a secret in that room. Whether that secret was the source of our current state was unclear to him, but he had his opinions.

My parents stayed for several weeks, not only caring for Maka and I, but for our patients as well. Working side by side, the community felt more comfortable and secure. We spoke of all things medicinal, and few things personal. My mother always felt that these things would come out in the right time, and they did.

It was in the early evening, after our last round of checking on patients for the evening. We sat together on the veranda sipping on hibiscus tea, discussing the different treatments we had been experimenting with. Seeking their knowledge, I discussed with them to four kinds of venomous snake found in our swamp. The diamondback and pygmy rattlesnake, the cottonmouth, and the coral snake. With many snake-bite victims each year, we were well versed in the use of button snake-root, a medicinal plant in the parsley family that was generally used to treat snakebites in many native American tribes. The coral snake generally attacked your nerves, inducing paralysis which would lead to a collapse of the victims' breathing functions. The Diamondback Rattlesnake was primarily a blood venom, preventing clotting and causing rapid internal bleeding. We discussed the various treatments involving snake bites with no clear resolution that would show the advancement of our knowledge.

It was Maka that spoke first about the Lwa. He introduced a theory that the combinations of traditional herbs, combined with the support of a spiritual assistance, could increase the effectiveness of traditional plant-based medicines. He positioned his theory as clinically as possible, but it still had an alarming effect on our discussion. Father leaned back; certain we were now talking about something entirely different. Mother leaned forward, knowing that this was the moment she had stayed in Cocodrie for the last two weeks. Both were silent, waiting for Maka to continue.

For the next two hours, Maka carefully unfolded his knowledge of Vodou, careful to discuss it clinically, not spiritually. He spoke of the Lwa. My Lwa was clearly Rada and his obviously Petwa. Although very different in their spiritual attributes, they were complimentary in medicinal practice. Maka was clear that he did not understand where the Lwa resided, or how they manifested in real life, only that he felt them when he called. He felt their guiding presence, and the amplification of their spirit through his hands as he treated.

Maka finished with the postulation that the Lwa, fed by sacrifice, and praised with dance and song, had allowed he and I to extend our treatment of all manner of illness well past that of my parents.

Mother sat passively for some minutes after Maka finished. Father put his hands on to his knees and stood with some effort, betraying his age and his years of hard work. "Tomorrow we shall meet your Lwa", he said. "And we shall see your methods". He took my mother by the hand, and they retired to Maka's room. Maka and I shared a single pallet bed. Still without intimacy, but feeling the need for closeness, for tomorrow was a critical test in our beliefs and our position in this village.

†††

Maka and I both started our day at the lagoon, fresh with the humiliation of being discovered in our past condition, washing, and preparing for our day. We broke fast with my parents and then walked the short distance to the hospital. No one waited, but we knew that would be short lived.

We led my parents to our ounfò. Pulling aside the curtain,

they spent moments looking over the alter. They saw the various herbs hanging neatly from the ceiling, the small brazier for boiling water for ritual teas, and the various tools of the trade, an ivory handled knife, a garrote, two cloaks of feathers and a single headdress made of feather and skin.

Maka introduced each of these items to our guests and then he draped the feather cloak over my father's shoulders and set the feather headdress lightly on his head. I draped the other cloak over my mother's shoulders, and we taught them the words of prayer before the alter. We lit the smudge pot, and we steeped the tea. As it readied, we instructed them in the Rada and Petwa. We gave them an idea of what to expect, and how to react. They drank the tea, and we held their hands while they entered the realm of the Lwa.

Through the day we admitted patients, treated, and then released them. No single injury or illness was significant, but in each I could see the Lwa working through my parents as they administered their care. I could see their astonishment and appreciation for the guidance and compassion their Lwa provided to them.

For four more days we worked side by side, instructing, teaching, and learning from each other. Four days of questions and answers. Of exploration and introspection. It was an enlightenment, and for people who are rarely surprised, they were astonished. We gave them the beginners primer and then sent them home to Dulac. Our single temple/ ounfò became two. Our Lwa were pleased.

True magic is not a sleight of hand, or a trick. True magic is an intervention by the Lwa to cause a result that would otherwise be seemingly impossible. The Lwa are like any human. They are selfish and curious. Demanding and greedy. They wield great power and possibility, but to obtain it, you must pacify and please them.

The drug allows the Lwa to possess you, the sacrifice buys you favor, the dance entertains your Lwa and ensures that you continue in this favor. Over the course of years, the Lwa becomes you. So familiar are you to each other that the lines between your human self and your Lwa self are barely discernable. You are best partners, compatriots, and companions. The Lwa counts on your attention just as you rely on theirs.

The magic begins as a favor. Your patient is losing their fight with life. They are taking their last breathes and you pray to yourself, "please give this man another chance. Please let him live.", and they do. It was your Lwa magic that brought this miracle. In exchange, you give up a small piece of your own spirit to the Lwa.

It could be in a small kindness. A young girl wants the love of an unattainable man. In fun your strike a bargain with your Lwa to make this happen, and it does. To you, it is only harmless fun, but each time you gain this magic from your Lwa, they own a little more of you.

As word spreads of your miracles, your favors become more frequent, and it becomes almost second nature to grant a wish or cure the incurable. Without even knowing it, your reputation is spreading far beyond your swamp. Beyond even the south.

†††

The man was old. Ancient even. He had traveled many miles from his home on the Eastern Seaboard. He traveled by train, then coach and eventually by palanquin. His men carried him through the swamp, through water and land. They had gone first to Dulac, but the magic was not strong enough. They continued to Cocodrie and waited at the hospital for Maka and I to arrive.

We listened to him talk of his illness and his need. He told us of his fortune if we healed him and the penalty if we did not. We were his last hope and if we could not save him from the grave, he would send us to ours. His men were heavily armed and serious.

Maka and I resigned to our ounfò and agreed that this threat against us was a violation of our sacred oaths and of our own persons. We discussed our options and then began our ritual.

Our headdresses were donned, a baby goat was sacrificed, and its blood spilled into a ritual bronze urn. We began chanting and singing to our Lwa, pleading for their guidance.

Our Lwa came to us with ferocity. Neither of us expected

this greeting and we were instantly on alert. While our years of working our Vodou had been a partnership of human and Lwa, we were now being dominated by these spirits. They were violent in their response to the man's demands, each in a different way. My Rada spirit was demanding that they were not a carnival trick to be demanded by any person. No man must dare to threaten a Oungan and Manbo of the Rada Lwa. The blood of these men be spilled into the swamps immediately.

Maka's Petwa Lwa was greedy and sinister. It demanded Maka heal this man and take his gold. Once the reward was in hand, the Lwa would then drag these men into a purgatory where they would be in torment forever.

Both Maka and I were shaking and sweating with fear. We babbled incoherently and spittle flew from our mouths as we attempted to regain control of the Lwa.

It was no use. We had foolishly tied our own spirits to that of the Lwa through many healings and rituals. We were now slave to them. For the next hour our Lwa communicated through us, arguing, fighting, and battling for the submission of the other. When a resolution was reached, our Lwa left us in a rush, and we collapsed to the floor. We were exhausted and covered in blood from the upturned bronze urn of goat's blood and the various scrapes, cuts, and wounds we received in thrashing about on the stone floor for this time. We lay panting, eyes wide and afraid.

†††

One of the Man's servants was first to enter our ounfò. Upon seeing us bathed in blood on the floor, and the strange accumulation of ritual objects scattered around the room, he quickly ran for help from his fellow guards. They entered the ounfò together, wide-eyed, and afraid of this scene. It was clearly witchcraft, an offense widely discussed by the devout in the North and prosecuted in the East. Together, they grabbed our wrists and drug us out of this den of Satan, and out into the daylight where the Man sat waiting for our preparation to be complete. Upon seeing our state, he had us bound and stowed in the hospital until we recovered. He would then see if our magic were good or evil.

As our bodies recovered from the efforts of our trance, we woke in our hospital, bound hand, and foot. The man reclined in his palanquin, smoking from an opium pipe, and watching us intently.

It was I who spoke first, as I shouted at the man for binding us. Maka was calmer, and he quieted me with a gentle look. All of this was observed by the Man who would be healed at any cost.

Maka asked the man what he was thinking, and the man replied, "it is you that should be answering that question. I ask you to heal me and I find you hours later laying in a pool of drying blood, cloistered in a shrine that seems to be to the devil. I am here for your magic, for no modern medicine can heal my cancer, but I must know if your magic is of God or of Satan?"

Maka looked squarely at the man and offered that he and I both needed to cleanse and relieve ourselves. Let us go to the river and put on fresh clothes, and we shall have a talk about Angles and Demon's. The man motioned for the guards to cut us loose, and they did so fearfully. It was clear that a man with no hope for recovery had no fear of death, but these men who were paid to protect feared us very much.

We walked straight into the river, clothes, and all. The blood had long since dried and as we entered the water, a pink stain formed around us. We immersed entirely and began the process of washing. Once our clothes were soaked through, we tossed them ashore and continued our cleansing. I could feel the lustful eyes of the men as they watched me bathe, but there was also a fear that that I knew would protect me.

Fresh clothing was brought from our home, and we dried and dressed in quiet. While this was taking place, the Man had a luncheon prepared from his own provisions. It included all manner of dried meats and cheeses, strange fruits we had not seen before. A whole dried duck was cut into bite-sized pieces, and we washed it down with a bitter wine.

The Man was patient throughout this meal, but you could see the impatience rising within him. He had few hours left in this world and every hour spent eating was an hour dying. Still, he was treading this issue very carefully. He had heard of possession by evil spirits that drove a man mad. As much as he wanted to be cured, he did not desire to spend an eternity of insanity.

Maka began speaking as he had done with my parents. He talked of the Lwa, and the blending of religions to increase the power of the spirits. He spoke of his experience with allowing the Lwa to enter his own mind and body. He spoke with reverence of the Lwa healing through both he and I.

Maka then did something I did not expect at all. He told

the man of our recent visit by the Lwa. He spoke candidly of the resolution to strip the man of his wealth, then drown both the Man and his servants in the swamps. All of this was taken in by the Man without emotion. Maka finished his conversation by telling the man directly that the Lwa had completely possessed him, and that he was powerless to deny the Lwa their due. Maka did not plead with the Man or speak out of fear for the Lwa. It was a matter-of-fact statement. If the man insisted on being healed by us, he would end up swimming with the alligators for his eternity.

Nothing was said for a long time. The man was shrewd and knew that he needed the Lwa to need him alive. Even if this was a fantasy or delusion, the Man must convince us, and our Lwa that he was valuable to them.

When the man at last spoke, it was in the direct, emotionless way he threated our lives upon arriving in Cocodrie. He simply said, "Let me meet them." And his fate was sealed in that moment.

While the man was confident of his ability to reason with the Lwa, both Maka and I feared what was going to transpire. We could feel in our bones that our Lwa would take this opportunity to eliminate the Man entirely. Maka had been very clear in his communication. There was no need to plead or beg for this Man to reconsider. He was warned, and now he would see the Lwa.

As we entered our ounfò, the servants talked excitedly among themselves. They had overheard Maka's description of the Lwa, and of their own impending death in the swamps. It is an unfortunate fact that the poorer and more desperate a man is, the more likely they are to believe in gods and devils. The witching stories of their home hearth were frightful. Each could clearly envision Satan himself rising from hell to drag them into the lake of fire for eternity. No sooner were we behind the close curtains of our ounfò, than the servants were running into the village to beg for help.

Society is a place where people congregate together. Such was the small society of Cocodrie. The people of this village had watched the change of Maka and I, from seemingly normal healers, to wild haired and filthy miscreants. Still, we were the only healers around, and our results were astonishing. We had developed an uncomfortable existence of necessity. They needed us, and therefore chose to ignore our eccentricities. Still, there was the creeping feeling that the situation would change in an instant should the consequence ever outweigh the benefits.

The moment the servant's rushed into the saloon, the situation indeed changed. As the servants described what they had seen and heard, the obviousness of our witchcraft became crystal clear. There was no need to investigate, for all the pieces that the community had tried so hard to ignore, fit together perfectly. The healers were wolves in sheep's clothing. No doubt, those that had disappeared in the swamps, as many did, were not eaten by alligators, or washed out to sea. They were sacrificed, just like the chickens, goats and snakes that had been found gutted and discarded in the swamps behind our hospital. While most become an easy meal for any number of predators, there are always those that are discovered by a hunter or wanderer.

†††

As our Lwa possessed both Maka and I, it was immediately clear that the Man had made a poor decision. Our Lwa, being so embedded with Maka and I, knew that Maka would share the entire. Like a cat playing with a mouse before eating it, our Lwa was playing with his victim. They were very clear in their intent from the onset of our possession, and we were unwilling slaves to their actions.

As the Lwa possessed the Man, he was filled with a sense of power and authority. They inflated his value and self-worth, and the man readily took the bait, being accustomed to this treatment in other parts of his privileged life. As the Man became confident, and even courageous, he issued demands instead of humbly approaching the Lwa with a request.

The Lwa allowed the Man to boast and brag, demand and order. Both Maka and I could feel the Lwa rising. We could feel the undercurrent begin to erode the footing below his soul. We could see the change in the man even before he felt it himself. First his voice faltered, his expression changing slightly as the niggling feeling started in his feet and climbed up his limbs like being dipped in wax. The confidence evaporated and the fear crept in. Slowly at first, then increasing in intensity. It was at this moment that our Lwa showed themselves to the Man. They appeared in all their terrible and hideous form. A form that we were accustomed to, and we understood to be kindred. Like the difference between a friendly puppy and a wild rabid dog attacking with froth and fang, our Lwa showed that they indeed had a terrible side to both personality and form.

They laughed their terrible laugh and drew out the skinny and scared soul inside this man. So emaciated was this soul, that it was clear it had little substance in life. As the soul ripped from body, the man's face twisted into abject terror. He desperately reached for the soul that hung midair before him like a limp rag. He begged and pleaded. He apologized and promised, to no avail.

Without his soul, the man was nothing. His physical form began to rot, like an orange left to the fungus, its form caving in on itself and shriveling. Was there physical pain? I do not know. I can assure you the spiritual and mental pain was excruciating. It was monstrous.

Outside we could hear shouting, and screams. Unknown to us, our Lwa had turned their bloodlust to the servants, as promised. As the horrified villagers looked on, the servants of the man suffered the same fate, and the same pitiful end.

The possession ended for us abruptly. Maka and I were released, and we stared at each other for long moments before we smelled the smoke. We rose on wobbly legs and exited the curtained ounfò. Our hospital was fully engulfed in flame, and we escaped out the back, over and through the open porch, wading waist deep in the swamp to escape the intense heat. Through the flames and fallen walls, we could see the villagers on the other side of the building. Torches in hand and fear on their face. There would be no talking our way through this. We would never be welcome here again. Maka waded to the rear of the saloon and found a pirogue moored on the beach. While the townspeople were occupied with their fiery duty, he filled bags with provisions. We slid the boat into the water, and within minutes Maka was poling us deeper into the swamp.

THE SWAMP

The Louisiana swamplands are a misery. Heat that is inescapable, humidity that leaves you drenched, even on the driest days. Swarms of mosquitos that envelop you as if in a cloud, piercing and sucking you dry of precious life blood, while simultaneously injecting you with a variety of viruses. It is a land of water, separated and segregated by fits and spurts of bog and dry land. Often, the water and land blend to make a soupy quicksand, or marsh. Cypress trees feature wavy, broad-based trunks. Their branches hanging down to the water, always thirsty. The swamps are a place of water broken up by odd lumps of land.

In the branches are every variety of bird life. In addition to the year-round avian residents, it is winter in the northern regions and songbirds by the millions come south to enjoy the warmth and abundant food in the bayou. Tens of thousands of birds per acre. Snakes, raccoons, and possums thrive here. They seek out and eat both egg and young bird as quickly as they are manufactured. Of course, the alligator feeds prodigiously on anything it can close its jaws on, as does the panther, who creeps silently in the wet grasses and abundant branches of the swamplands.

Hunting is not an issue in the swamp. There are plenty of eggs that do not hatch, or the stillborn or young chicks that are forced out of the nest by siblings greedy for more of mother's catch. It adds up, alligators get about 40% of their annual diet from outcast eggs and chicks.

Of course, both panther and alligator also feed on the wayward human adult or child that is not paying attention. Human meals are generally those who are injured, snake-bit or pass from one of the many illnesses carried by mosquito. Once the decomposition of the body starts, these predators will sniff out the corpse and feast. With no body left to claim, the imagination is left to wander about the hoodoo, voodoo and ghost that might have crept into their homes and drug them to hell under a full moon.

Maka and I boated deep into the swamp, deeper than we had ventured prior. Maka had only recently buried Augustin Hebert, an old swamp veteran who had outlived all his neighbors and had finally succumbed to a stomach flu that left him dehydrated and malnourished. As fast as he ate, it drained right out of him. His body held no nutrient and he essentially starved to death sitting at a full plate of food.

Maka had a good idea where his home lie in relation to Cocodrie, but in the swamp, there are no straight lines. We ambled this way and that, driving deeper into the glades. The sun was setting, and night is not a good time to be drifting in the swamps. It is the time of the predator, and we both looked intently for any sign of cabin or shack. We almost missed it, for it was built back into the wood, up on a hilly knob, and surrounded by cypress. Were it not for the low-slung dock stretching a mere fifteen feet out into the bayou, we would have slipped right by.

Maka poled the flat-bottomed boat up to the dock, and he stayed while I reconnoitered the cabin. We could only imagine we had come upon the Hebert domicile, but it was unwise to walk up on some of the more militant Cajun people nearing dark. The lights were out and I haloo'd from the shore before approaching the cabin. I peeked in the windows to make certain all was safe before letting myself inside. I lit the oil lamp by the door and did a short pass through the cabin to insure it was indeed Hebert's, then returned to the dock to help Maka bring up our supplies. As a final task before the sunset full, we moved the pirogue up the shore and tied it under the low branches of a cypress.

The home was remarkably clean and well apportioned for a bachelor of some years. It was one large room with a solid home-made bed, a rock fireplace, and a solid roof overhead. Augustus Hebert's clothes would fit Maka, if only slightly large in girth and short in arm and leg. The kitchen was in a lean-to out back, as was a pit toilet. Maka checked the toilet to ensure no varmint or snake had moved in during Augustus' absence. When our inspection was done, I set about making the broth for a bisque, while Maka took a net to the bayou to catch a few fish for dinner. Catching dinner in the bayou was a simple as throwing out the net and hauling it in. One toss provided us with a dozen redfish. Maka picked out four fish and returned the rest to the water. He quickly filleted the fish on the shore, leaving the entrails and bones for the scavengers, and he washed the fillets in the bayou before traipsing back to the cabin.

I tossed the fillets directly into my broth and allowed it to simmer while I looked through Augustus' trove of herbs. I selected a few and tossed them in the pot and along with some dried heart of the saw palmetto and a wild radish known as betony, we were able to make a hearty broth to bring a comforting end to a rather disturbing day.

Barely a word had passed between Maka and I since leaving Cocodrie. Even through dinner and to the bed we would share, we said not a word. Today was for thinking, tomorrow would be for talking and decisions. As the oil lamp was snuffed, and we lie in a strange bed, I wondered what this would mean for my parents in Dulac. I wondered what it meant for Maka and I.

†††

"Hoo dere?" came the strong masculine voice from down bayou way. The voice stirred us from our deep sleep, but neither of us had a chance to gain our bearings and respond before the voice came again, this time closer, and more insistent, "hoo-dere?".

I threw a smock over my slip-dress and stepped out onto the veranda, the pale morning light just rising, a mist covered the bayou. A man with scrappy, torn coveralls and several days growth of beard stood not twenty paces from the house. He held his pirogue pole in both hands, in a menacing way. "Hoo be you" he asked.

I replied that I was a friend of Mister Hebert. He stared a long time, apparently thinking of a response.

"Hebert, he tell you come do"?

"I am the healer from Cocodrie," says I. "Mister Hebert passed away and left me his home", I lied.

The man's face told me what I needed to know. He had already heard of the passing of Augustus', and he likely knew the story of our flight from Cocodrie, even though it was news only hours old. News had a way of traveling quickly through the bayou.

"It's a nice domicile," he said, using the Cajun word for home. "Mebbe I keep it for mesself?"

It was then that Maka came to stand by my side. The man knew well of the stories of us together. The miracle healers of Cocodrie. The strange, possessed two who were likely murderers.

Maka, in a voice that was calm and welcoming asked the man to please come and join us for a morning cup of chicory. He responded by returning to his pirogue and fetching redfish and crawdads, which made a delicious gumbo. That morning, we got to know Marcel Guidry, and he us.

Marcel spoke with great reverence to the memory of Augustus Hebert. The two had often hunted and fished together. It was Marcel who encouraged Augustus to seek us out in Cocodrie. "Da man were not well. I fear he would die, and 'da man did", said our guest. I explained the nature of his illness and we all agreed that he had a good life in the bayou, and he had built himself a fine home on this high ground.

We invited Marcel to take from the house what he would, he being a friend and helpmate to Augustus. He loaded his pirogue full of things he could use, topped with the fine bentwood rocker he had always coveted. Before leaving, he said that there were others who would come claim their own keepsakes. Such was the way of the bayou. We did not need to ask him to keep our secret, for he would not. We knew that the people of Cocodrie would not seek us out here except for healing, but they would not harm us, nor would they tell those who might be in service of the Man where we were to be found. The swamp keeps its secrets. Every man must live with his conscience and his actions, until his own death.

†††

Come they did, two to claim possessions from the Hebert home and four who needed healing. When one is ill or wounded, he rarely worries over the moral code of one who can heal them. This would often be followed by their spreading of gossip and lies about the witches of the swamp. This was not my first experience with the true hypocrisy of humanity, but it was a tiresome occurrence.

Each time a story is told, there is a small amount of modification and manufacture to the telling. The words become more descriptive, the actions more inflated, the story grows with each telling until it no longer resembles the facts. Such was the tale of Maka and I. As the villagers of Cocodrie explored our ounfò and poked through the graveyard of animal skeletons behind the hospital, the stories and assumptions grew beyond any form of reason. Yes, Maka and I practiced a very different form of religion. It invoked spirits that were both good and evil. We had been consumed by these spirits to the point of losing our own selves. These things were true, but the stories that came out of Cocodrie were of sorcerers that sacrificed animals and children, to achieve the miracles and mystical healings we had produced. Our possession was not a partnership with our Lwa, but a possession by the Devil himself. To be healed by us was to join in pact with Satan.

And herein was the hypocrisy. For even as the words left their mouths, when they themselves needed healing, they would come to our door under cover of dusk for their potion or curative and leave before the last rays of sunlight passed over the bayou.

†††

A time did come when men came looking for us. We did not hear of it until long after the alligators had feasted on their carcasses. There is one constant of the swamp. It takes care of its own. Even though we were among the most marginal of peoples tolerated in these swamps, we were indeed people of the swamp. We were a part of the water and land like any cockroach, water moccasin or hermit human that lived here. Every person residing this far south was feared, as much for their ferocity as their life choices to stay. No man in his right mind would live in this hell. It was only natural that we stand together in our oddity. We were a community of outcasts, and we protected each other like brothers and sisters.

The men came from the deeper water. They arrived in steamship from New Orleans, steaming down the Mississippi river and out into the open water at Bootheville. They traversed west into Lake Barre and skirted Bay Cheland until the water became too shallow. They offloaded seven Pirogues and with five men each, they poled up the East Bayou to Cocodrie. There they provisioned for an extended search of the bayou. After their money was spent, and the locals told them a few bare faced lies about where to hunt, they set out to find Maka and I.

We would not be found in the East where they traveled, for we were nested in our cabin in West, in the Bay de l'Ouest. This is a most inhospitable place for any creature and only the heartiest and determined would stay. We were not the only residents, for among the mangrove and Spanish Moss there were hundreds of similar cabins, each housing humanity that was as rejected as we. So remote were we that we could go weeks without seeing another soul. So hidden was our cabin, years could pass before anyone knew we were hidden in the shadows.

The intrepid expedition of armed men was hired by an agency from Atlanta. They wore bowler hats and vests of wool. Their boots shiny and black, their guns carried at the waist or in a holster at their shoulder.

East they went, back to the Bay Chaland, then up into Bay Negresse. They searched for weeks until they found the entry into Bay Lucien. By then, their guns were badly rusted, their woolen vests tossed overboard, and their boots replaced by bare feet. Their hair hung wet in their eyes and their white cotton shirts were stained and brown under the arms and down their backs. Their hands and faces were pocked with a thousand mosquito welts and some eyes were swelled shut. They were in misery, yet they were paid to do a job.

They traveled in circles, in and out of the mangrove. They first questioned locals, and when they did not get the answers they wanted, they began to beat them. Word traveled fast to avoid the men from the North, and for days following, they saw no man.

Illness spreads quickly among men huddled in close quarters on boats. Bayou virus is carried by both rats and mosquitos. It brings fever, headache, and a host of neurologic manifestations. Rarely fatal, but it compounds an already miserable and uncomfortable journey. Four men had already been lost to snakebite and alligators. Two more died in fights over food or petty arguments. Tempers were high and patience was low. In frustration, the men returned to Cocodrie with murder in their heart. They had been played for fools and had paid dearly.

In their haste, they had tried to cross open water of Bay Negresse during a storm. These flat bottom boats were only suited to the shallows and seven boats became five. In Bay Chaland they lost another, and now their troop numbered only fifteen. They poled into Cocodrie a ragged group of men. Each twenty pounds lighter and half-starving. They fell from the boats at the marina, their legs refusing to hold them up, and they crawled and staggered to the saloon, where the saloonkeeper took the last of their coin in exchange for cooked fish and watered wine. With food in their belly, and their confidence returned, they began to threaten the locals with violence. A final round of drinks on the house, served by the saloonkeeper, paired with a bowl of what he called beach apples, slowed what was becoming a dangerous situation. The wine was drunk, and the men tucked into the fruit. Its sweetness was quickly followed by a peppery feeling in their mouth. As they swallowed, their throats burned and tightened. The beach apples come from the manchineel tree, also called little death apples. Touching this tree can be fatal and eating the fruit definitely so. And so succumbed the fifteen, who were then mercilessly dumped some quarter mile away on a mound of earth simply know as crocodile mound.

The village gifted the quick-thinking saloon keeper with the five pirogues, and the townspeople and visitors split the various possessions of the men among them. Within a few hours of their arrival, there was no evidence of their ever having arrived.

This was the tale as it was told to Maka and I less than a week later. We were very familiar with manchineel. The wood had been cut and allowed to dry in the sun to neutralize its poisonous saps for decades. It made sturdy furniture. Through our experiments with native plants, Maka and I had devised a way to turn the saps into a gum resin that would treat edema and process the fruits to cure constipation. As has been taught to us, all plants bring health to us, we just need to determine how to use them.

THE FORBIDDEN LOVE

Healing in the Bay de l'Ouest brings fewer patients, and less trade. We now needed to augment the food and necessities of trade for medical assistance with foraging, hunting, and farming for ourselves.

Our staple was the redfish that was ever-present. There are berries, fern, saw palmetto and other plants that grow everywhere. There are white-tail deer, plenty of alligator, and birds abound in the trees and on the land. Gathering food is not a problem here, but it consumes every minute of every day. When you are not foraging, you are cooking, or cleaning. When the sick or aggrieved come to our door without something to trade, we will often need to make them wait while we provide for ourselves.

I say aggrieved because those who are healthy are coming to our door with greater frequency. They are people who are not coming for healing, but for magic. They want a love, or a curse. They desire wealth or companionship. They want and want. They are willing to seek us out in the furthest reaches of civilization to get it.

Often enough, we provide what they want. We have needs ourselves. We desire things that only money or trade can provide. Our want for these things demands we provide certain services in exchange. Potions for love, extracts for facial blemishes, restoratives for hair and wealth and power in their own small worlds. While we charge a fee of our service, the Lwa extract their own payment. Such is the way of Lwa that we can only assume that wealth will come by marriage to an abusive spouse, or power comes over something trivial and undeserving. Restoring hair may result in impotence and love might be unrequited, driving the one possessed by our charm into madness. These things we do not see, for once we complete our transaction, they are gone, and we do not see the results of their folly.

But still they come, so somewhere, someone is telling the story of our magic. Someone is boasting of their power over love, hair, or money. To us, with our swamp cabin, and the clothes on our backs as our sole possessions, they are as insignificant as hair on a frog.

How does this magic come? You know how the healing happens, is the magic the same? It is not. Medicine is very serious business to the Lwa. It is the culmination of their power and control to cure and heal. The magic is entertainment. It is a parlor trick where the asking party becomes the butt of the joke.

It always begins with a quest. The Lwa will accept sacrifices of small animals for healing, but for magic the Lwa demand something more exciting. The person asking for the magic must provide a sacrifice of the Lwa's choice, and it must be caught by their hand.

A wealthy spinster from Baltimore sent an expedition into

our swamp to procure a love potion. They were sent home to return with the spinster herself. Imagine a woman of great sophistication and wealth traveling by carriage south to Chauvin, Louisiana, then by cargo boat on the Bayou Petite Gallou, south for fifteen miles to Cocodrie, where she must stay two days in the saloon before a boat can be arranged to take her to our cabin in the Bayou de l'Ouest. Madame Elain Duroir arrived disheveled. Her wig askew and windblown. Her voluminous dress and petticoats drenched with swamp, sweat and mud. Her jewelry was lifted from her in Cocodrie, leaving her hands and neck bare. The woman was barely keeping herself together, but she was desperate.

We welcomed her to our home and made a restful place for her. I gathered her garments and washed them in the bayou. They were now a lighter shade of yellow, but they would never see white again. I begged her to leave the layers of petticoats off to assuage the heat and humidity, but she said something about femininity and the necessities of a lady, and that was the end of the discussion. She wanted her magic, then to leave immediately, but the Lwa are not so simple. They have demands of their own.

She took our bed, and we slept on the floor nearby. She wrestled with the heat and insects all night. She feinted when a snake traversed her bed to get to the other side. She cried herself to sleep, only to wake minutes later to sob some more. Little sleep was had by anyone that night.

The next morning, she woke to chicory coffee, redfish and the last of our lentils. She picked over the fare with veiled disgust but ate most of it. We had left her men to find their own food, which made them surly and argumentative.

The first order of business was the passing of the coin. We had learned long ago that magic rarely left the client filled with gratitude and benevolence. Most often, they ran from our ounfò, and were never seen or heard from again. Madame Duroir was not to be trifled with financial matters, and her financier counted out our required price into my hand. Once secured, we dismissed all but Madame Duroir and began preparations.

We led her to our ounfò, where she stared wide-eyed at the shrine we had built. It was far more elaborate and intricate than the ounfò at Cocodrie. It was littered with bones and feathers and pots filled with various incenses. It smelled divine, and she swooned at the magic that permeated the air.

Because she was lucid and aware, were obligated to tell her, in detail, what she could expect. We also told her that not even we could predict how the Lwa would greet her request. We were clear that the Lwa were serious about medicine, but often played those looking for self-indulgence for fools. She bristled at being called self-indulgent, but let it go with little more than a scowl. When she arrived, she had been almost desperate for the magic. Now that she was here, in this moment, the excitement seemed to have turned to boredom. She wanted nothing more than to fulfill her travels and return home.

We placed the feather headdress on her head, a human femur bone in her left hand and a handful of seed in her right, then began to dance slowly around her. Our body rhythms were slow and exaggerated. She held her hand aloft without passion. She was limp with boredom, and not at all entertained by our dancing and song. Even if she were, she would not give us the satisfaction of showing it. We swayed and dipped and shuffled our feet across the dirt floor. As our dancing increased pace and intensity, her eyelids fluttered closed, and sweat began to pour down her forehead like a waterfall. Her fists, filled with their possessions, shook mightily, clenched until her knuckles were white. Her breathing was deep and gravely, her breasts heaving under the layers of cotton.

Then her eyes opened wide, and the dancing stopped. Not a muscle moved. No sound was made. Slowly, a look of desperation crossed her face. She was puzzled. Confused. She looked to Maka and said, what is a Greater Siren?

†††

Maka and I sat talking throughout the day. The Lwa had demanded the sacrifice of a Greater Siren, and Miss Duroir was to fetch it and conduct the sacrifice personally. There were two problems with this demand. First was that the Greater Siren was one of the most elusive creatures of the swamp. A giant black salamander, slimy and slithery. It would be difficult to find, and nearly impossible for her to catch. Still, this was her magic, and both Maka and I were content to allow it to play out as the Lwa willed.

We sent a boy to fetch Temmy Rowan, a well-known fisherman and swamp expert. If anyone knew where and how to catch a Greater Siren, it would be Temmy.

Madame Duroir sat in a chair on our porch, chain smoking with trembling fingers. They moved nervously about, virtually destroying the hand-rolled object before it was half smoked. Maka offered her some of his herb to smoke, but she turned her nose up and dismissed him, and his offering.

We had explained to her what a Greater Siren was, and the challenges with finding it. She called her financier and told him to pay whatever we demanded to fetch the salamander, but we quickly dismissed the notion. This was her magic, her quest, her offering. She alone must complete this task. The financier had not seen the Madame in our ounfò. He felt that we were charlatans and fakes, trying to swindle the Madame of her money, but one look at the young woman told him that she had encountered some form of vision. It frightened him, and he quickly dismissed himself to the porch where he poured one drink after another for hours.

Temmy arrived in the early evening. He shared a meal of alligator tail etouffee and brought a bottle of store-bought wine. He negotiated a rate with Madame Duroir and agreed to take her out the next morning. Long after she had retired to a restless night's sleep, Maka, Temmy and I talked about the quest, and what perils the city woman may be in for. Temmy was not at all concerned. He knew of a place where the Greater Siren nested. It was shallow water where they could be herded into a net of fine satin and trapped with ease. He wanted to know why the hell this city woman wanted a Siren, but we did not discuss magic and sacrifices with the locals. It was bad business and he seemed to understand that the less he knew, the better.

By dawn, I had a small kerchief parcel with leftover tail from the night before and clean water from our spring in a gourd. We saw Temmy and Madame off. Her guard nervous and uncomfortable allowing their ward to be taken into the swamp with a heathen, but she insisted. They brooded about before returning to an early day of bread and whiskey.

Temmy poled up the Bay de l'Ouest and into the bayou. He spoke not a word, and she made not a sound. She became enraptured by the varieties of creature and plant seen from this small craft. In her shrouded carriage, she had not seen anything but the enclosure. Here, the entire world was both open, and closed, for the swamp is simply an endless series of living corridors, mixed into a labyrinth of turns. She had no sense of direction, no idea where she was, and if Temmy had died on the spot, she surely would have perished as well.

While he never spoke, Temmy did point out all manner of life. The roseate spoonbill stork, with the obscenely long legs and a bill flattened into a spoon at the end. He pointed out an alligator, swatting it on the head and driving it deep in the mud below. They had wiped her head to toe with sweetgrass to minimize the mosquito pestilence, and it worked. On her way to the Bay de l'Ouest she looked like a marionette, swatting endlessly at unseen mosquitos. Today, she barely registered interest.

She shivered on the many occasions when Temmy pointed out a cottonmouth snake. She had a deep aversion to lizards, snakes, and all things crawly. Since she did not know exactly what a salamander was, she still had little concern, and she did not want to show her ignorance by asking. She would cross that bridge when they came to it.

In early afternoon, Temmy found a suitable hummock

of dry land to put the boat upon. He offered his hand to Madame Duroir to get out of the boat, but she refused, and promptly fell backwards into the swamp. Temmy had offered and she refused, and he would not now assist her with climbing out of the water, wet as a rat.

Seething, but hungry, she dropped to the ground, demanded Temmy fetch the lunch and sulked until he had spread their meal before them.

It was in this one, small moment of quiet and intimacy that Madame Duroir began to ask Temmy about his life here in the bayou. Why would he choose to live here when there was a great, beautiful world out there for him to enjoy?

For an hour, Temmy spoke of his beloved swamp like a poet laureate. He praised plant and animal. He spoke of the symbiotic nature of all living things as clear as a scientist because he was one by training. He was in fact a man of Harvard who had come to the bayou some twenty years earlier to study the botany of this remote place. He never finished his thesis, and he never completed his education. He never left the swamp. He was home, and he had spent twenty years documenting, categorizing and cataloguing thousands of new species of plant and creature for posterity.

Madame Duroir was enraptured. She said not a word during his long discourse, but when he was done, she was quite taken with this balding mountain of a man who smelled of sweat and fish and masculinity. She wanted to tackle and take him in that moment, but she was here to win the love of her Oliver. A man of wealth and position in Boston.

As for Temmy, he thought Miss Duroir a silly, spoiled girl.

She could not cook or clean. She did not know how to care for herself in this place. She was a novelty, an entertainment. Not unlike the women he had chained to the porch of his domicile in the past. There was a darker, more terrifying reason Temmy Rowan found comfort in the solitude and seclusion of the swamps. Temmy looked for runaways or homeless to bring to his swamp home. Although he would very much like to take this woman down a peg or two, he was smart enough not to invite suspicion on to himself.

They continued for another hour, nearly within sight of the Wax Bayou when Temmy poled the boat up into a small creek of freshwater. Here, they departed their pirogue and waded in shin-deep water into the interior. Temmy led the way with a machete, deftly cutting away the vines and dead-fall that would block their path. He dropped his rucksack and fished around to remove two objects. The first was a thin willow handle with a bentwood hoop. Attached was a delicate net of fine filament. So delicate, it could have been woven from beautiful, long blond hair, which of course it was. Miss Duroir asked about its manufacture and Temmy replied that he had made it himself. It was a special net made for catching elusive creatures like the salamander. He placed it in her hands, and then he assisted her in wrapping her hands around the handle, mimicking a smooth sweeping motion. It goes like this, said he. She barely heard a word. His strong hands over hers, the thick muscles of his forearms, golden brown by the sun. She swooned and caught herself as he asked if she understood. She did.

Together, they waded into the stream. He several yards

below her. She planted the net, hoop-side down, in the water, resting it on the stony creek bed. He crawled on hands and knees, digging his fingers into the earth, dislodging, and chasing anything on the creek floor upstream towards the waiting net. Good fortune was with them, and she felt the net jostle with movement. As he taught her, she swept the net forward, raised it, then spun it, closing off the top. Water poured from the sieve, and they could see the black, shiny body of their prey inside. Temmy took the net and opened it, looking inside to see two Greater Sirens inside. He asked the lady if she would like to see, but she declined. She had her prize and would entrust Temmy to ensure their capture until they returned to the ounfò. She wanted nothing more than to return to the Bay de l'Ouest and be done with the entire affair.

Temmy gently urged the Sirens from the net into a wet burlap bag, which he tied tight and set into the bow of the boat. He then picked up his pole and they began they journey back to the Bay de l'Ouest. Madame Duroir sat in the back of the boat, watching the still, brown water pass underneath the boat. Despite the distractions that the swamp environment held, she could only think of the broad, brown back of Temmy Rowan. The fibrous muscles moving under a stained sleeveless shirt. The unexpected intelligence of what she had assumed a roughhewn man. She was enraptured and could not escape her fascination.

It was after dark when they saw the blazing bonfire signaling the cabin. It had been a very long day and Madame Duroir passed on supper and headed straight for her bed.

Temmy, Maka and I talked over fried raccoon, purslane,

and cabbage palm. Temmy recounted the day's events, then lay down next to the fire and slept. I took off my evening shawl and placed it over him, grateful for his kindness and assistance. Maka threw a few chunks of wormy wood on the fire, and we turned in for the night.

Despite her exhaustion, Madame Duroir would not sleep well tonight, for Temmy Rowan haunted her dreams with visions of passion and pain. She felt the sting of his whip, and the edge of his blade as it carved lines into her skin. Lines into which he rubbed soot from his fire, making permanent tattoos across her body. In her bed she writhed and jerked in fear. She begged for mercy, then begged for more. So conflicted was she, that she woke herself many times during the night, each time sinking back into a slumber haunted by more dreams. Over and again until daybreak found her red eyed and weary.

†††

Madame Duroir (for she still had not invited us to call her by her first name), was ravenous and of ill humor as she stormed through the house. She did not speak a word during her morning meal. She headed directly to the ounfò when done and waited for us there. She was on the edge of sanity. She had come for the love of a sophisticated and cultured man from Boston, she had dreamed all night of a coarse man of the swamps. Only her stubborn nature kept her on this foolish course.

Maka and I wordlessly dressed her in the ritual headdress, and placed the bone in one hand, and the Greater Siren in the other. Her scream startled us all. Maka and I were already entering a dream state, her bodyguards and porters were idly milling about the fire pit outside. Temmy, accurately assumed that the city woman had finally met the salamander, stood, brushed off the dirt from his filthy clothing, and sauntered over to the ounfò.

Her porters, bodyguards and financier burst into the ounfò, guns out and ready for a fight. Maka and I were stifling laughter as Madame Eileen Duroir, the toast of Boston society clenched the seven-inch-long salamander so tight in her fear, that she squished his guts out both his mouth and his ass. Still screaming, and still clenching, Temmy brushed everyone aside and gently pried her hand open and discarded the dying Siren. She looked at him, desperate for him to hold her tight and calm her, but he was a man of the swamp, and not a gentle or nurturing person. He shook her firmly until she broke into great heaving sobs.

When she settled down, Temmy produced the second Siren. She stared at it for a long time, afraid to reach out. Maka gently told her that it was too late to turn back. She had made a contract with the Lwa. She must fulfill her end of the contract.

With all standing around watching, she reached out and took the creature in her hand, and gently closed her fist over it. She was fighting the bile in her mouth to stay down. She trembled with fear and revulsion. She looked up into the eyes of Temmy Rowan and found no comfort or support, only a cold, expecting stare. A week ago, she would have dismissed the look and moved on to others who would pacify her for the attention and money it meant for them, but today she wanted only for Temmy to notice her. To take her into the swamp and make her his own. Temmy's expression clearly told her that he could care less about her comfort, and that only made her want him more.

I ushered everyone out of the ounfò and Maka began the ritual. Even before I joined in the dance, the Lwa were already there. They had been watching with such joy and hunger. They had measured this woman and found her to be petty, shallow, and unworthy of their magic. Her willingness to go into the swamp with Temmy was commendable, but her killing of their sacrifice before they could enjoy it was a final straw. She had come for magic, and they would deliver it.

The Lwa knew exactly what kind of monster Temmy Rowan was. They could see the calm, educated exterior, and the fierce, brutal man underneath. They could see the bodies of women weighted with rocks surrounding his small cabin in the swamp. While the Lwa had no respect for men such as Temmy, they thought him to be a perfectly suitable punishment for Madame Duroir.

The Lwa possessed both Maka and I with a fierce vengeance. We were shocked at their entrance but dared not interrupt the ritual. We could feel the sinister side of them fully display itself. On the demand of my Lwa, I produced a small scalpel to Madame Duroir. In a trance, and completely helpless, she cut away her blouses until her bare breasts lay exposed. Here, with eyes closed and head thrown back, she scrawled the name of Temmy Rowan into her chest. Not deep, and not large, but legible. Even in our own trance-state, Maka and I exchanged a glance of concern. We were all in this moment at the whim of the Lwa. As a final act, she brought the salamander to her chest and sawed his head off over her breast, allowing the thick, viscous blood to run down over her. It seeped into the carving on her chest, permanently marking her as his property until her dying breathe, which would likely be in a few days' time.

Madame Duroir had found her man. She had entered into a magical contract to have the absolute devotion and love of Temmy Rowan, and indeed Temmy would be devoted to her for the next few days. He would love every minute of the remainder of her life, then her would discard her like all the others, sinking to the bottom of the swamp.

It would take Madame Eileen Duroir two hours to become fully conscious. There was no evidence of the cuts she had made on her breast, nor of the blood. Only a feint, thin scar that was visible to those who knew what to look for.

We helped her to her feet, and she seemed not to notice that her pale, white breasts were exposed to all. I quickly tied her dress up in a makeshift manner. It should hold until she could change, but she never did. We walked her into the sunlight, and she walked directly towards a startled Temmy Rowan. She took him by the hand and led him to his pirogue. She pushed the craft out into the water, and taking up the pole in her own hands, she began poling them to deep into the swamp.

Maka and I watched alongside her staff as they drifted out of sight. The men looked about each other, trying to determine what was happening. They waited for two days for her to return, and when she did not, they packed up their own boats and head north towards home. As they left, the birds, insects and animals seemed to have taken a short break and the silence was beautiful. One by one, the swamp life began their soft symphony until the world had returned to normal.

LWA

The ritual of Madame Eileen Durior changed the dynamic between Maka, I and our Lwa. No longer were we temporary vessels of these healing spirits. They took up a permanent residence in each of us. We became the human embodiment of these great and terrible wraiths.

Once completely inhabited, we lost our sense of self, and became what we were before my parents found us, a feral and filthy host for the spiritual world. This had a tremendous effect on all who came to us for healing or magic. From their first moment with us, they were terrified. They would beach their boats and walk up to our porch. Although each had heard what we had become, nothing could prepare them for their first impressions of us. We did not skulk or slither about like snakes like they had heard. We walked upright, with absolute power of presence. Wild hair, wild eyes and filth covered our naked bodies.

We did not ask them what they came for, we told them why they were here. We knew their souls' days before they arrived, foretold by the Lwa who were biting at the bit to have fresh sacrifice and dance. They cared nothing for the visitor, only the celebration and sacrifices we offered, for this is the feast of the Lwa.

Once arrived, we would demand payment before we would hear of their reason for visiting. Payment was determined by the clothing they wore, the servants in tow, or the absurdity of their request. Swamp locals were still offered a barter or trade, but the city folk paid in gold or silver, and we had more than we could use, but a price must be negotiated and paid before we would help them.

There was also the issue of the sacrifice. Locals knew to bring a gift for the Lwa, but city folk were instructed to go find a worthy sacrifice and return. Temmy was ever-present these days. He had made a business of taking our clients into the swamps for their sacrifice. Occasionally, the Lwa would give a greedy woman to him as a prize, so Temmy made an extra effort to insure the Lwa sacrifices were more than worthy. Without a sacrifice, they were sent away and told to return when they had the full fare.

The money passed hand, and we commanded them to our ounfò. They would attempt to explain their reason for coming, and we would be putting on the ritual feathers and taking up the dance while they still stammered on about their ache, be it physical or emotional. Wide-eyes and shaking, they were in great fear of the wild witches from the swamp. Terrified, but not so much as they would leave. Some did, but most stayed on to the bitter end.

In our current ever-possessed state, the Lwa were present immediately. They encouraged our dance and chanting. They wondered what special treat Temmy would supply, and when the sacrifice was bled, the Lwa would have the visitor drain the blood over our heads and bodies. In their spirit state, they could not feel the blood, but all spirits want to be as close as possible to the sacrifice. We hated this part. The blood got into our eyes and our mouths. It was metallic and thick. We were incapable of denying the Lwa anything.

The day came when a man named Josiah Thistlewaite came to our squalid hut with a young son of ten years named Adam. The boy had suffered a massive blow to the head and had become a simpleton. He drooled from the corner of his mouth and his head hung slack. His entire body looked like a set of clothing hung from the line, limp and lifeless. Josiah was greedy, and selfish. He did not want Adam healed for the boy's sake, but because the boy was an embarrassment to his business. He tried to have Adam committed, but they would not take him. We were the final hope. We were to cure this boy so he could take his rightful place in the family business, proud and intelligent.

You can only imagine how this effected the Lwa. So many people had come to us seeking health of an unhealthy child. The most innocent and honest lives. These people would gladly lay down their lives for their children. We asked little of them other than to love their healed child when they left. This was the benevolence of the Lwa working through us, and we were glorified in this act of selflessness.

But this was different. We knew that if we failed, this boy would never make it out of the swamps alive. The father would leave him to the wilds to perish, then make up a story for the benefit of business and social sympathy.

It is a fearful thing to feel the wrath of the Lwa. It is far more fearful to feel the calm of unemotional disgust and hatred. There was only one logical solution. Without benefit of sacrifice or dance, we took Josiah's gold and placed the cloak over his shoulders, and the second cloak and headdress on the boy. Without preamble, the Lwa possessed both at the same time, giving the boy the man's vitality, intelligence, and health. With it was full knowledge of what the father had done, and what he would do if the boy was not healed. Josiah Thistlewaite, in turn, received the boys broken mind, but with enough of his own to understand what was occurring. It took minutes. And the ritual was over. Maka and I had not even participated beyond a few formalities. This was the work of the Lwa.

Adam Thistlewaite, now of sound mind and body, assisted his broken father to the water's edge and helped him into the boat. He pushed them off, and without a word of thanks, he paddled out into the swamp and was lost to the glades within a few minutes.

This is not where this story ends, it is a new beginning, a new chapter. The Lwa, in their arrogance, had become the judge, jury and executioner of all who came before us. They blessed some, cursed others, but always at their whim. As they possessed Maka and I, they had only our spirits to show them the nature of humans. They had not experienced the true cunning and deviousness of humanity. They would now.

†††

During this time, on the Eastern seaboard of America, religious zealots were flexing their moral muscle, claiming those who did not conform to be all manner of witch or sorcerer. Although nearly all were innocent of the accusation, they would be tortured until they confessed, then killed for their confession. This was not the first time this occurred, for 100 years prior, the witch trials occurred, and the stories were still told, and the embers of fear were always red with opportunity. Even earlier, both Catholic and Christian churches had executed many in various inquisitions. It was trial by pain to determine guilt, but the accused died whether they were guilty or not.

The process began with an accusation. It was generally one landowner who wanted the land of a neighbor, or a woman wishing to steal away the man of another. Claims of witchcraft were made with the church. The church, in its greed, would require payment of a dowery to accept this accusation and declare guilt. Thus, the church made a tidy profit of accepting accusations, then attacking the innocent with the full anger and ferocity of the Catholic or Protestant church, whichever happened to be accepting the coin.

The accused was rounded up and brought before a tribunal. Evidence was brought by the accuser, but the accused was rarely allowed to speak, instead, they were subjected to a series of tests, which they would not possibly pass. In their failure, they would be put to death in the most heinous fashion, for sin was thought to be purified by pain.

This practice would end in the early 1700's, but in rural Mississippi, men took their religion seriously, and did not easily let go of folk tales and myth. Mississippi had joined with the rebels in driving the British out of the Orleans territory in the early 1800's, but the Territory of Orleans belonged to the Houma Indians until 1812 when the Territory of Orleans became the US state of Louisiana.

In Jackson Mississippi, they were itching for a fight, any kind of fight. Adam Thistlewaite was heading home to deliver it. He had a plan, and he wanted power. This was his chance to take it.

This brings us back to our selfish benefactor whose son was saved. In their haste, the Lwa had not considered the mental state of the son prior to his accident. As it were, the Adam Thistlewaite was far more sadistic and devious than his father. He was, in fact, violent and murderous at times. He was hungry and desperate for power and would likely have killed his own father for the inheritance in short time. But the Lwa had done the job for him, and he returned to his home with a fresh evil in his heart.

Although the boy had no religion, he knew to engage with both the Catholic and Protestant churches. He wanted to create an event, with him at the center of attention. He wanted to use his event to vault him into the political arena. This was the best opportunity he would have.

He ushered his father to the Catholic Diocese. The priest's welcomed Adam with surprise, for the last time he was seen, he was but an idiot. The older man, who was known about as a scoundrel, was now the idiot child. Was this a miracle of Christ, or something sinful and evil?

The boy spun his tale in truth. He described being led into the swamp, with his father's intention of healing or killing him. He went into detail of the Sorcière and their sorcery. His story would crescendo with his father's mind being crushed and his own restored. While he was grateful, this was a sin against God and all men. These Sorcière must be rooted out and displayed for all men to witness the horrific nature of Satan. The Priests were riveted to the conversation and understood the value of this testimony to his church as well. There was great profit to be made with a demonstration of Satan's work being cleansed by the Church. Knowing the boy was heir to a fortune, the Priests asked for their fee to accept the accusation, but it was the boy who demanded a fee to show the Church where these witches lived. The Church, still seeing a mighty profit, agreed, and the coin changed hand.

The boy would sell this tale to the Protestants and the Lutheran congregations. Each was competing for followers, and the tithes and money they delivered. Each unknowing that others had already purchased this information, all ready to use this information to create a charismatic renewal of faith. A common enemy was found, and they would root it out for the sake of all mankind (and for a solid profit).

Of course, the churches quickly discovered the betrayal, and they accosted Adam Thistlewaite in the streets, determined to call out his sin in front of the community, but young Mr. Thistlewaite stood his ground and declared that he had packed and was ready to lead an army of God's true followers into the swamps of Louisiana, and to return with the Sorcière for a very public trial. Adam had stolen the center stage. It was he who was seen as the great leader, not the Christian Gods. In resignation, each church fell into lockstep, calling on their devoted to join in this crusade.

Seventy-five men and women climbed aboard a train of wagons, headed south-west. Forty-two would return.

†††

What should have taken twenty-two days to reach Houma, became over thirty. Every town they went through had to hear the tale and get riled up, for Adam Thistlewaite was fighting for recognition and notoriety. He could parlay these into a leadership position in a new government. This was his key to greater riches and more power.

Thistlewaite needed every town to rally behind him and at each stop, he would stand in the back of a wagon and preach a Pentecostal fire and brimstone sermon about the evils of Satan, and the witchcraft done just a few miles south in the bayou. He rallied the troops, and each stop yielded a few more men and women to his growing army of God.

At Houma, they rested for a week while Adam preached daily in the street. At five-thousand residents, this was the closest city he would encounter on the way, and it would be his last chance to solicit the faithful to join him.

There had been much progress in overland travel in the last many years and wagons were able to travel south through Ashland, all the way to Dulac, connecting the swamps of the south to commerce in the North.

In Dulac, the massed army of God, some 200 souls, unloaded from their wagons in front of the hospital. Adam Thistlewaite called out to my parents to come out. With some curiosity, they did, standing before this mass of people as caregivers and healers. Adam Thistlewaite ordered them to be captured and bound, accusing them of witchcraft. He sent followers to uncover their ounfò and used the contents to bolster his accusation. There, with his army threatening any who would interfere, Adam Thistlewaite ordered my parent to be hung from the cypress tree that shaded their hospital. As the bodies jerked and twisted, their Lwa awoke too late, and before they could exact their revenge, my parents were dead, and the Lwa no longer had a connection to this world. Adam Thistlewaite had won the first battle.

With bloodlust coursing through their veins, the assembled confiscated every pirogue, boat, and skiff they could find. The locals were too few to fight back, and they seemed to know that there would be a reckoning when Adam Thistlewaite gripped with the witches of the swamp.

The group sought out guides, and several came forward, but when they determined each was only luring them to their death in the swamps, Adam Thistlewaite determined that he would use his memory to find their way back through the swamps to our home in Bay de l'Ouest.

The flotilla of pirogues, led by our representative hero who attempted an impression of Admiralty, left Dulac under the sweltering August sun. The boats launched with the gathered singing hymns and cheering on their quest. Two weeks later, Adam Thistlewaite once immaculate clothing was now tattered, torn and soiled. Every inch of skin not covered by clothing was a mass of welts from the hordes of mosquitos and stinging insects. His fingernails were deeply inset with a layer of black, loamy earth and his long, luxurious hair was a knotted nest, resplendent with twigs and detritus from many nights sleeping on the boggy shores of the glade. His gathered were a glum mirror of himself. Many had either perished or deserted, their faith shaken by the reality of the swamps. They were 128 when Adam Thistlewaite emerged into the Bay de l'Ouest and cheered the tenacity and faith of the remaining.

A renewed spirit arose, not for the battle to come, but at the prospect that soon this would be over, and everyone could return home to a more pedestrian life.

Maka and I had received plenty of warning. In our ounfò, and within possession by our Lwa, my parent's spirits came to us and described in detail the tragedy of Dulac. The combined Lwa would make us a much more formidable response, and Maka and I invited my parents Lwa to join with us. We could now feel the combined energy of these Lwa. We were fools to believe we could harness and contain them. Now they had force, power, and a human container to hold them to this world. If we were simply possessed before, we were now owned by these Lwa. We would not simply be protecting our domicile and way of life; we would be decimating an opposing army. Maka and I quickly resigned to his new fact and began preparing in earnest for the arrival of Adam Thistlewaite.

For days, between treating our patients and foraging for food, we would discuss with our Lwa the situation. The Lwa were full of pride and power. They were seemingly unconcerned about the amassed group heading towards us. Nothing we could say would bring them to engage with us on the subject. They would need to see the threat before they would recognize it for what it was. They did not understand religious fanaticism. They had witnessed only human frailty and greed. They would soon see what blind faith could create.

††
†

The afternoon was hot and humid. A slight breeze did nothing to assuage the discomfort. With bellies full from their morning meal and knowledge that today would be their day of salvation, Adam Thistlewaite and his remaining army paddled and poled their way out of the bay and up into the bayou that was our home. As they rounded a bend in the river, they could see all the way up into our spit of land. Although our domicile was well covered by branch and vine, Adam Thistlewaite knew it was there, and we knew they arrived. We stood in the shadows of our dock, at waters edge. Maka armed with a machete we used for harvesting herbs. Its blade was two foot long and razor sharp. I held my own machete and had a long fisherman's pike pole planted point first in the soft earth beside me. We would defend home and hearth, with the help of our Lwa.

Adam Thistlewaite stood in the bow of the lead boat, tired from his travels, but far from beaten. Behind him was his revived and frenetic hoard. Only a day prior they had been beaten down, uncertain and ready to go home. But today, they were seeing the witches in the flesh. They could feel the vindication of their cause, and the superiority of their belief over those who had turned back premature.

Maka and I stood still as stones, for we were completely under the control of the Lwa. They were not divided in their opinions about the outcome of these new arrivals. They were of singular mind and spirit. We could feel the Lwa slithering and comingling, like water pouring over itself. Theirs was a celebration of the violence to come. It was a unified front.

As Adam Thistlewaite stepped upon our dock, I stepped to the right, walking along the shore, then stepping into the water, knee deep. Adam Thistlewaite noted my movements but kept his eyes resolutely on Maka. Maka smiled a black-toothed grin and welcomed the return of Adam Thistlewaite with his friends. With gentle voice, Maka asked how we might be good hosts?

In his infinite self-obsession, Adam Thistlewaite walked toward Maka while proclaiming that he was here with God by his side. A chorus of amen's and blessed-be's were heard from the assembled. "We have cleansed Dulac of its satanic evil" he said. "Now it is time for us to cleanse the swamps of its demons and restore all to the glory of our blessed Lord". While the assembled prayed and wept and cried out their blessings to their God, Maka and I stood still as the cypress around us. Our feet rooted into the wood of the dock, and the mud of the bayou. Behind Maka and I the visage of four Lwa were slowly rising into view.

Adam Thistlewaite hesitated. He had completely forgotten or glossed over the facts of his miraculous healing. He had chosen to replace the fear of Maka and I, and our Lwa, with a foolish memory of his own bravery and release from his mental shackles. In this very moment, it came rushing back to him. We were not just filthy swamp rats, we were powerful people, with powerful spirits aiding us. If we were capable of witchery on he and his father, what other things might we be capable of? A sweat broke out on his forehead, and he stopped dead in his tracks. The last thing he would see was the pale outline of our Lwa, surrounding the head of Maka as the machete sliced clean across Adam Thistlewaite's throat. Our hero dropped to the wooden slats of the dock with a slap and a splash of crimson. The gathered looked on in disbelief, transfixed by the unbelievable violence before them. They were here as emissaries of the almighty God. They were here to hang these demons and then go home to their families, children, and communities as hero's. Now, their leader was struck down without so much as a whisper of resistance.

So intent were they on Maka, they did not register the sweeping arc of my own machete as it cleaved through the neck of a middle-aged woman, nearly beheading her. I pulled the blade towards me, and in a single graceful arc, chopped downward into the neck and shoulder of the man sitting next to her in the pirogue. Maka and I, driven by our Lwa, worked our way from Pirogue to Pirogue, pulling bodies into the water, and slicing, chopping, and hacking our way through the assembled while they frantically attempted to back pole their way out of our reach.

Our victims were not the only ones afraid. The terror I felt was absolute. Maka and I stared at each other the entire time our bodies were attacking the faithful. We had no control over our movements. We were completely engulfed in the spirits of our Lwa. We knew we were lost, and we felt the end of our lives culminating in this moment.

For Maka, it would be more than a symbolic death, for a random shot from a pistol caught him square in the forehead, completely by chance. All four Lwa quickly abandoned me and rushed to his body, attempting to fix the mortal wound. This left me visible and exposed. I was covered head to waist in blood and gore, staining the dark waters around me. The remaining eyes of the invaders fell upon me as they frantically fought to pole their boats out into deeper water. They could see the horror on my face as I regained control of my body, but they were beyond their own terror. They were in full panic as they sought the safety of the swamp.

A shot was fired, then a second. I stood feint and weak as the bullets tore past me. None hit the mark, and soon they were out of range to try again. Without looking back, they quickly poled north to the nearest opening in the swamp, and they were out of sight within minutes. Many more would die before they found their way to Houma. Once there, the story of the witches of the swamp spread like wildfire.

As for me, I was free of the Lwa. While they worked in vain to revive Maka, I pulled my way over the rail of the nearest pirogue, wrestled the bodies into the swamp, and poled west, deeper into the swamps.

†††

Maka and I were innocents. We had harmed no one. We had been the savior of many, and the ruin of those who used us for ill purpose. Yes, we had invited the Lwa into us for many years, but it was an innocent possession, never intended to harm, only intended for healing. Yes, we had taken it too far, and in our naiveté, we had given our Lwa was the power to possess us and enter into this mortal world. Yes, I was likely responsible for my parents' death, and the deaths of all those that were currently feeding the alligators, panthers, and fishes in the swamp.

But there was also an inner conflict. Had the Lwa led

us into this danger, or had they protected us against it? Yes, Maka was dead, I felt his life flee from his body the instant the bullet struck home. I knew I did not possess the power to resurrect what was dead, but the Lwa, they may have had the dominion over death. In that moment, I did not stay to find out. Without my Lwa I was both liberated and terrified. For the first time in my life, I was entirely alone. I felt stripped bare without the protection of my Lwa, but I had been given the chance to escape, and I had taken it.

I was thirty-two years old, and alone in the world.

BAYOU CHEVREAU

The swamps are filled with jagged coastlines, and I could have made good time by simply poling across Moncleause Bay into Caillou Lake, but I wanted the security and safety of the swamps. I hugged the jagged coastline. Should I be followed, I could quickly slip into the swamps and disappear. Out on the lake I was exposed and in danger. Besides, I was in no hurry, for I did not have a destination. I simply needed to put distance between myself and the rest of the world.

Leaving Bay de l'Ouest, I poled my bloody pirogue for days, drawing a steady column of alligator behind me, targeting the scent. Those that got too close received a swift tap with the end of my pole, driving them underwater, but never far away.

As the birds fly, the distance across Caillou Lake is less than ten miles, but the following of shoreline tripled that distance. Lift the pole and drop it into the muddy bottom of the bayou, push down and back, shuttling your craft forward. When the pole is nearly out of your grasp, you pull it from the muddy bottom, lift it through the water, and repeat. Pole over pole, moving westward across Caillou Lake. Through the talk of visitors, I knew that Lake Merchant attached to Lake

Caillou by a thin waterway. This was my only direction. Pole over pole. I sleep in my pirogue. I eat from the provisions left by my predecessors and augmented my diet with the plants the swamps offered to me. Highbush berries, elderberry, black alder fruit and multiflora rose all are found in easy reach of a passing boat. Inland are the garden pea, watercress, skirret, butterbur, and black chokeberry.

I pass through the waterway into Lake Merchant. The muddy black water of Caillou Lake is augmented by the pale greens of Merchant. I pass through and hug the shore to my right. Quickly the water turns brackish and black as I skirt Mud Lake. It is completely undrinkable, and too close for comfort. I continue and then chance an open water crossing to a small peninsula where the water immediately lightens. I follow it Northward into what I will learn is Bayou Chevreau. I am immediately taken with the desolation and remoteness of this place. The Spanish moss that hangs from the cypress seems luminescent. Springs of fresh water run clean from the mounds of earth that make up the shore. How clean water can exist in this tea-stained and muddy world is beyond me, but it is here, and I welcome it. I stop and drink my fill, sitting alert on the mossy bank and watching the several alligators that float off the stern of my pirogue.

The only truth of the swamp is that it is never quiet. There are always alligators growling, frogs barking, crickets chirping and birds singing, squawking, or crowing. To the uninitiated, it can be maddening. I had lived a lifetime in the swamps and so my maddening moment came when all noise in the swamp suddenly ceased. Not gradually, but abruptly. Not even a stirring of breeze. It was so quiet that it hurt my ears to strain for any sound at all.

He came to me as an apparition, a ghostly visage. Hovering over the water, just feet from where I now say. It was Maka, with a clean, round hole in his forehead. Around him was a fury of four Lwa, trapped within his dead body. Our Lwa were demanding I sing the songs and dance the dances that would release them and bring them into me. I was afraid, for I knew what the Lwa could do, but I was also free, and I chose to deny them. I said a single word to them. "Go". I felt them leave my consciousness entirely. My body and soul physically shrugged off the weight of years of possession by these beings. I was free for the first time in my adult life. I did not intend to ever let them back into my life, but we life does not always play by the rules we wish.

†††

I lived alone in Bayou Chevreau for two years. I found another abandoned cabin, although one not so grand and solid as they one I had left. I gathered the large, ruffled palm leaves and shingled my roof to keep out the rain. I anchored them with leafless vanilla vine. I searched for two days to find a suitable slab of bark to make a functional door. I cleared the birds' nests and reptiles from the old fireplace and found a single cast iron skillet that was badly rusted. I scrubbed it with sand and a wooden staub for a half day until it was clean enough to cook from.

My final task before settling in was to bathe. I did not need a reflecting glass to know that I was a terrifying sight. The looks of those who came for Maka and I in Bay de l'Ouest told me volumes. It was the same look I witnessed in my parents faces when they had come to Maka and I in Cocodrie. I looked at my arms, at the dried and caked human blood, days old. It was caked under the very same fingernail of the hands that picked the sweet redfish meat from the bones that I ate every night. Without my Lwa to cloud my mind, I saw myself clearly for what I was. A crone of a Sorcière, not yet thirty-three years old.

I made a roaring fire of dry cypress next to the water and packed twenty double-fist sized stones around the flames. I then dragged my pirogue up onto shore, with the widest end downhill. I shoveled water into the back of the boat with my cupped hands until I had several inches of water inside the stern. Only then did I wade out into the swamp to get as much dirt and muck off me as possible. I scrubbed my skin with sand, removing much of the flesh, but not all the filth.

I waded out of the swamp, the brown-stained water running off me like a heavy tea. Although the sun was already beating down, hot and humid, the evaporation of the water sent gooseflesh up my arms as I dried in the open air.

Using two hollowed out sticks, I carefully lifted each hot rock and deposited it into the water in the pirogue. Each rock warming the water in my makeshift bathtub until it was hot enough to melt away the oils and greases in my hair and skin. As I gently lowered my body into the warm water, I instantly relaxed. It seemed ages since my body had released this tension. I would occasionally step out of the tub to remove cold rocks and replace them, or to scoop more water in. I had pounded some pinecone ginger into a mush and thoroughly scrubbed my hair and scalp with it. I let it set for twenty minutes while I slowly worked on the rest of my body. I would occasionally run my fingers through the snags and snarls of the tangled mass my hair had become, working the ginger through the strands, and coaxing out the tangles.

When I simply could not stand the warm water any longer, I waded back into the swamp and rinsed the mushy ginger from my hair. With the mush came the oils and dirt, leaving my hair long, soft and refreshed. I could not remember the last time I was this clean, and it felt good. I twisted my hair to squeeze out the excess water and coiled it atop my head as my mother had done when I was a child. I felt reborn.

†††

Mother had often told me of the difficulties that pilgrims and settlers had with freezing snows and the agony of hunger, but in the bayou, we knew neither. Although the weather was either hot, or hotter, we always had plenty of food. The game was plentiful, and easy to catch. The plants grew everywhere. If you knew what was safe to eat, you could never grow hungry here. Even when the hurricanes and big storms came and swept through the glades, knocking down trees and uprooting all manner of plant from the sparse land, there was still an abundance.

No freezing and no hunger, but the hurricanes were no laughing matter. In Dulac the hurricanes were terrible, but Dulac had miles of bayou between the Gulf of Mexico and the town to soften the blow. Cocodrie was terribly exposed, and each hurricane required much repair of homes that were damaged, or even swept away. Bayou Chevreau was by far the most protected homesite I had in my memory, but that first year produced the most horrendous storms, and my shack barely held together. My new shingled roof was nearly tore off, much of the siding disappeared in the winds. All the herbs and medicinal plants I had harvested and dried were a soggy, worthless mess. I would need to start all over, and so I did. I would have the same results the next year, and so I began searching for a better domicile.

Men have been populating the swamps and glades for centuries. There are all manner of shacks, domiciles and huts scatted anywhere you find high ground. Some of these looked prehistoric and primitive, just sticks and mud. As I moved northward, I often would stay in these old huts as moderate protection from the wild things outside.

I traveled for miles, poling my pirogue up a promising finger of water, only to dead end and turn back, looking for another break in the swamp. You might look in thirty or forty fingers before you find one that opens into a waterway. I traveled north, and slightly east up a good, wide opening. My eyes searched left and right for any sign of domicile. The watery path would taper to a dead end, and I would back up and look for another path. This type of travel is tedious and endless, but to me it was also a fascinating puzzle.

Twice I found good domicile's that were occupied. No one was there, but the fresh footprints on the shore and wet fish nets were telltale. I kept moving. I was encouraged, because I wanted the company of others, but I was afraid, because I was a pariah and an outcast even to the outcasts. I was an outlaw in a lawless country. Fair game for anyone who took offense to my presence.

On the third day I saw clear sunlight ahead, a good omen in the cloistered darkness of the thick jungle foliage. I approached, as always, slowly and with caution. It was good that I did. The finger I traversed opened into a large canal waterway, a full two hundred foot across. Lining both shores, above and below me, were shacks and domiciles of a medium sized town. I searched my memory but could not remember a town being here. Trouble was, I was much farther East than I had thought, I was in Dularge, just a stone's throw from Dulac. Over the last many years, I had traversed a large circle, coming back near to the home I had known years before.

I quietly and quickly poled back the way I had come, determined to stay close enough to this town to be useful, but far enough away that I would not be part of the community. I would need to be careful.

†††

I poled in and around the glade for two more days before I found a suitable domicile to occupy. Frankly, it was the dock I found, mostly covered in vine and leaves. Unused for at least a storm or two. I tied off my pirogue, and scouted for the trail, which was faint, but discernable. I hiked up the trail and out into a meadow opening. The meadow was large, a good three acres in size, much larger than any I had seen in the swamps prior. The meadow switchgrass was tall and thick, reaching to my waist, but easy enough to walk through. I ferreted out the path up to the domicile at the top of the meadow.

Once again, it was well built, but in severe disrepair. I

harvested a long, thin log, and a short thick one and fashioned a lever. Placing the thick log close to a sagging wall and situating the long log over the top of it, and under the base of the wall, I was able to lever the wall up a good four inches. I had fashioned an anchor from some vine and a sturdy rock outcropping to fix my lever, and that allowed me to backfill under the wall with stones and rabble that would serve as a make-shift foundation. I repeated this around the cabin until it was fairly level.

Next, I set about closing the holes in the roof with palm fronds and vine. Again, not a reliable fix if the winds came up, but it would buy me time until I could buy an axe in town to make shingles. I had scavenged several nets that had been abandoned throughout the glade and sat on my porch mending them with the crude stone tools I had, for I had not even a knife to my person. I had left every possession in Bay de l'Ouest in my hasty retreat. Still, I was resourceful and young. I could do for myself.

†††

Years later, I poled my pirogue into Dularge. No one would recognize the tall, lithe woman poling alone as the haggard witch of rumor, but they were curious about a young woman poling alone into town. If there is one thing you should know about bayou villages, it is everyone knows everyone. A stranger was uncommon.

I did recognize one or two people from Dulac, its proximity to Dularge was close and it was reasonable that through marriage or opportunity, some would end up here. I was fortunate to have changed dramatically since the days spent in

Dulac. No one suspected that I was the daughter of the murdered healers, but the story was likely still told in the saloon and social gatherings.

I was swift to trade the herbs and edible plants I had collected in my bayou for a few meager necessities. I was in town little more than forty minutes before I was poling back to my bayou home.

The following day, Olber Montague poled up to my dock. He landed his pirogue, and stepped out of the boat, turning to remove a large cotton sack from the craft and proceeded to walk up to my home. I met him at the door with my newly purchased knife in hand. He stood a respectful distance off from the house, removed his worn and stained hat and held it over his heart and offered his name and that he thought I might appreciate some store-bought food. He left the sack on the ground and turned back to his pirogue. As he poled back in the direction of Dularge, he turned, smiled, and doffed his hat once again before poling out of sight. I had neither a positive nor negative feeling about Olber Montague. I felt neither gratitude nor appreciation for the gift. Everyone is wary of a stranger, and in this meeting, we were strangers to each other. Most gifts come with strings attached, or expectations. I had not asked for this gift, nor would I acknowledge it to Olber Montague, but the canned peaches I ate on my porch were the sweetest I had ever tasted.

Olber was not the only caller. Over the next week, different men would seek me out, exploring the routes others had taken. Each returning to the bar to brag about their courting of the strange woman living alone in the swamp. The barroom talk included descriptions of the roots hanging from my porch to dry in the sun, betraying me as a healer. Each brought a gift, and each left with me still holding tight to my knife.

One had shown up drunk and demanding. He had walked right up to me on the porch with a black-toothed grin, looking me up and down in my homespun cotton dress. I would lose half a day to dragging his body to the water's edge, hefting him into my pirogue and poling him deep into the bayou where the alligators and wild cats would feast on his corpse. The long-jagged gash across his throat is where my arm shot out and slashed without warning. I betrayed no emotion or surprise, for this was who I had become. I had seen what men like Temmy and this unknown drunk could do to a woman. I would give them no opportunity.

Months later, it was not a man that came to my domicile, but a woman. I did not recognize her, but she had recognized me the minute she saw me in Dularge. She was a homely, hunched back woman in her early 30's. Likely the progeny of incestual family members. She moved with a jagged lurch, and it was plain to see there was pain in this movement.

She came with a flour sack full of food, but she also came for the Sorcière she knew I was. She would keep my secret if I could help her. There was no pity or fear in her manner. She did not beg or plead. She talked straight and plain. This was not a negotiation, but a bargain between a witch and a desperate woman. She would not take no for an answer.

I motioned for her to join me on the step of my porch, for it was the only place to sit. I told her that, although I had possessed magic before, that it was lost to me now. The woman reached her hand out and placed it over mine, staring deep into my eyes the entire time. I could feel the warmth and comfort of that light touch. I had never been touched with tenderness in my adult life. Maka was a friend and partner, others were simply clients and due only my pity and service. This woman, with her flaws and desperation, was showing me pity and compassion. My eyes welled up and I fell into her, holding on tight and sobbing with breathy gasps. She held me tight, gently cooing that all would be alright. In her Cajun dialect she whispered, *"Pauve ti bete"*, poor little thing. She would take care of me, and in turn, I would take care of her. It was not a request, but neither was it a demand. It simply was. And that is how Coy Doucet came to live with me.

Coy was patient. She set about taking stock of the domicile and its contents. She made a mental list of things we needed, and she left for two days to fetch them from Dulac, not wanting to cause gossip in Dularge or Cocodrie. We spent a week working on the cabin to make it habitable for two. The large cotton sack full of sheep's wool was the first bed I had known since my time in Cocodrie, for since, my bed had only been leaves and soft bark strewn on the floor. We shared this bed together, holding each other close in a sisterly manner. We would wake spoon to spoon, with an arm around the other. It was comforting and safe.

Each day Coy and I would venture into the swamp to gather medicinal herbs and plants. I would gather up beggartick flowers and I would point to my head and joints, showing its pain-relieving value. The ever-present aloes, whose mucilage flesh soothes burns and heals scrapes, but is also an effective laxative. Wormseed is boiled down into a thick candy that is effective against intestinal worms, which are prevalent among the freshwater fish diet of most residents in the glades. A tincture of calendula relieves bruises and strains. Gelsemiun is a depressant and mullein is effective against irritated skin. Every plant in the glades seems to have a medicinal value. To the uninitiated, it can seem like magic when a potion is properly prepared and administered, but it is just nature taking care of her own. Real magic comes from the supernatural. It is always present, but rarely called upon, for when magic is used, there is always a price to be paid beyond currency.

As memory of the witch healer began to wane, Coy began spreading news of a new healer in the bayou, and soon there was a steady clientele, come for healing. When people are in need, they ask few personal questions. A few were curious, and there was talk in town, but if pressed, I would dismiss those who would gossip without care, and so they learned to mind my privacy.

They came with their snakebites and their malarial fevers, wounds, diarrhea, infections, and sores. From each, a price was paid, whether it be in food or currency, did not matter to me. Some offered help, and that is how my roof was repaired and a fence was built to keep a few pigs that were payment.

In a place with few healers, it was inevitable that some of my old clientele would eventually find their way to my door. They saw before them a woman of forty who looked sixty. Clean groomed, hair brushed and thickening in the hips and breasts. I vaguely resembled someone from their memory, but they rarely saw the wild and crazed woman they had known years before. Besides, the faithful who had escaped the massacre of the witches some ten years prior insisted that both witches were killed by the hand of the lord himself.

I played dumb, claiming to have been in some other part of the bayou when that horrific event occurred, and only come to this place afterward, when I learned there was need for medical assistance in this remote part of the world. Whether they believed me or not, they paid for their healing and moved on. Although privacy was highly valued in this place, so was the need for news and gossip. The old stories hung in the air like a fog, transparent, while still being tangible.

I discovered that many of the healings I had relied on the Lwa for in the past, were completely within my own skill and knowledge. The Lwa had become a crutch that I found I no longer needed. True, not all people who came to me survived, but there were none who had died that I cared for so much that I would invoke the Lwa to return. My own safety and security were worth more than anyone who came to my door.

Coy's condition deteriorated as she aged. She walked with a sturdy stick and hobbled on aching joints. Her sleep became increasingly restless, as the pain in her bones was unceasing. It was obvious that her patience was near its end, still, I knew that she was beyond my healing ability. Only the Lwa could save her, and even Coy, with her companionship and assistance was not worth that price to me. Coy was less a companion than a security. If she was pacified, her threat was minimal. Coy was simply a ghost in my house. Ever present, but insignificant unless she proved to be a danger. So far, her demands were simply a nuisance.

The day would come when Coy's patience had run its course and she demanded of me to heal her. I started to explain the futility of her request, but she slapped my face hard enough to startle me, but not enough to hurt, and made her demand. I would heal her, or she would leave me. With clear threat, she sealed her demand with the promise to carry my secret to Dularge, Cocodrie and Dulac. I would need to run again. I was once again reminded that children could form friendships, but adults could never be true friends. There was always an expectation or a demand. With resignation, I told her that there would be a terrible price, likely far worse than the physical price she paid daily. She understood and was willing to pay any price to have her burden lifted. I told her a price would be extracted from me as well. She turned and walked away, oblivious to any consideration for my comfort. She had paid her price in companionship, now I needed to produce her healing.

There is a saying as old as time itself. *Be careful what you ask for, you might just get it.* Both Coy and I would have done better to think on this before we took this too far, but she was desperate for healing, and I was desperate to maintain my privacy and keep my identity. We were at an impasse. I was tired of running and had found a home in this place. I would not let go of it without a fight.

It took me a full month to prepare for what must be done. For a full week, I sat in the bayou in solitary, I drank from the clear creek, I ate the sparse jerked meats and seeds I had brought with me, and I thought about every possible option and consequence. At the end of the week, I made my decision, and I was prepared to live with it.

The second week was spent gathering herbs and roots alone. I would not allow Coy to join me, and in this she became curious and uneasy, as I had never refused her company prior. During these forays, I sought out hiding holes and hidden places. The third week I spent caching provisions in each of these places. The time had come. I sent Coy to Dularge for provisions, telling her to be as stealthy and obscure as possible. *Do not draw attention to yourself, for the work we must do must not be interrupted.* In truth, it was impossible for Coy to be obscure. Her hunched lurching drew every eye, as I had intended. Coy's insecurities also demanded that she brag on the most recent healings we had conducted together, for she counted herself as my assistant, and therefore a vital component of the healing. No visit to Dularge by Coy would be a quiet one. She would spend her last two hours in town at the saloon, drinking the homemade liquor they distilled, and telling half-truths about her life with the medicine woman to whomever would listen. When she had run dry of money, and was awash in liquor, she would stagger to her pirogue in erratic fashion that was all too common in Dularge, where the drunkard outnumbered the sober three to one.

I was in my pirogue waiting for her on the Southern shore of Lake DuCade. I bid her to follow, as she had so often done when we harvested in the Bayou. Instead of poling west to our home we headed south, into a dark, hidden network of rarely traveled canals and bayou. After some hours travel, we docked our pirogues on a slippery, muddy shore. We tied my pirogue off to low hanging branches and then drug her pirogue ashore. This was low-land swamp. Most dry land was simply a short spit of dirt separating more swamp. It took us no more than twenty minutes to drag her boat over the slick mud and moss spit to the other side, where we slid the pirogue back into the water. Coy was accustomed to such travel and asked no questions as we poled through heavy cypress and vine. We would do a land crossing twice more before we were at the halfway point between Lake De Cade and Jug Lake. This was deep swamp. It was a place where perhaps no human had every tracked before I had scouted it the week prior. It was ancient and foreboding, but Coy could see rare medicinal plants that we had often searched. No doubt her curiosity was piqued, but she remained stoic as I poled her deeper into the thicks.

I poled us up onto a gator, slide. A place of slick mud where the alligators would enter and exit. Surrounding the slide was Herbe á Malo, sometimes called lizards tail. We would pry up the herb, roots, and all, with a short, sharp spade and it would come up in clusters.

Coy struggled to bend her knees into a comfortable position where she would harvest all round her. Once settled, she pushed the point of her spade into the soft, loamy earth and pried back, lifting the soil, and exposing the bone white root underneath. She stared as red drops of her blood sprayed across the root and leaves, My rusty knife, honed to a razor-sharp edge over the last several days, drug smoothly across her throat and up the side of her neck to the artery, unleashing a gusher of blood.

In her last moments of conciseness, she realized that my betrayal was a gift. A release from the pain and discomfort of years. An escape from the whispers and laughter of strangers. A death in a beautiful place where her remains would be scavenged quickly, but where no human would ever disturb her eternal rest. As life left her body, she stared at the dirt, moss, and small flowers of the Herbe á Malo, as they slowly went out of focus. And then she was gone.

I left Coy where she lay and slid my body into the swamp to wash in the dark brown water, stained by a million years of decomposing leaves. I said a small prayer to whoever was listening for Coy, returned to the boat and backed away from the shore as a granddaddy croc came to investigate. I poled away with peace in my heart. I felt no remorse, only relief. For ten years this threat had been held over my head, and with one swift motion of my knife, the threat was gone.

THE RETURN OF THE LWA

Yes, time has passed. It is not measured in days, but in years. I lived alone in that place. My place. I cared for the sick with absolute devotion. I was a servant of the bayou, and was generally seen as a helpful spirit, despite the rumors and gossip that would persist over the decades. It was a time of peace and of loneliness. There was now a known route to my home, and time had worn a path to my front door.

This is not to say that I was without fear, for a woman alone in this place knows all manner of fear. Even the healer needs a healer on occasion. The swamps are filled with predators of all kinds, some slither on their bellies, some walk on four legs, but the worst are the two-legged variety. I have been hunted, stalked, and abused by men over the last fifty years. I carry a long batón whenever I leave my home. It is tipped by a steel machete blade salvaged from the pack of a man who had died on my kitchen table, which still served as both my meal-place and my surgery. The blade is rusted, but sharp as the tongue of a harpy. It is a useful tool as I cut through vine and bramble to collect herbs, but more so as a warning to those who think me a helpless woman alone. More than one ruffian has left with his blood on my staff, or left where he lay, to become a meal for the scavengers of my land.

But even the edge of my blade was challenged on the day Temmy Rowan appeared in the meadow below my home.

†††

Temmy Rowan. A man who had realized great benefit from Maka and I so many years prior. A man we never feared, for he was our clean-up, our protector. But the years had turned this studious scientist who lived in two personalities, into a singular vicious one. I could see the man at the bottom of the meadow from my porch. Like so many before him, he struggled with every step, and every breath. It was clear that he was wounded, but I did not raise from my chair to provide assistance. If he made it to my home, he would be cared for. If not, nothing I did would likely have saved him anyhow.

But come he did, and it was nearly twenty minutes of struggling before he was close enough for me to recognize. He was older, much older. Most men never achieve longevity in this place. The glades are a place of youthful death, not old age, yet here we were, two aging, broken bodies, holding on to our lives by hook and crook.

When he reached my porch, he looked up at me with ragged, rasping breathe. He managed to cough out a greeting, " bon ami, healer". He slowly dropped to the ground, leaning against my porch post until his labored breathing evened out. We sat in silence for a spell before he spoke again, back to me, never turning to look. "It was a tragedy what happened to your black fella. He was a good healer, and a good man. I have heard many versions of the tale; none painted the two of you in a good light. Heard you was dead some years back".

We sat in silence for a while longer before he said "The constable done catch up with me. I butchered one too many women, and the policeman was the cause of my current wound. I'm done out, witch, said he.

I could see the blood pooling around his bare feet. His blessur, or wound was such that it had been bleeding for perhaps several days. It would not be a small wound, and he would need mending.

I stood and walked through the doorway, knowing he would follow when he could. I stripped my table of eating utensils and put a clean sheet of coarse burlap on the table. It was itchy and uncomfortable but would sop up some of the blood as I worked. I was more concerned with my ease of clean up than of the comfort of a patient who clearly was asking for trouble. Yet who was I to cast a stone? With a rare moment of remorse, I tossed a stained cotton sheet over the burlap.

I could hear Temmy struggling to get to his feet, then the slow ascent of two stairs, then the stagger into my domicile. I helped him on to the table and went to work. I cut away the filthy shirt to reveal a bullet wound low on the abdomen. His entire belly was covered in deep blue bruising. I carefully felt around the entry site, hoping to feel the lead ball close to the surface, but there was no such luck. It was buried deep, and he was bleeding internally.

I took a small cypress stick wound in rawhide from its resting place and placed it between his teeth. He knew exactly what this was for, but he never showed fear or anxiety. He has seen that look on the face of every woman he had beaten to death, and he did not want to feel it himself, so he simply blocked it from his mind and acted as if this were the most casual and routine examination. His façade crumbled and he screamed from deep within his soul as I stuck a filthy, dirt-stained finger deep into the bullet hole to feel for the lead. Now his eyes were wide and fearful. Sweat broke out on his brow and his breathing became guttural, feral even. I smiled. Temmy was not a friend, although he was an acquaintance from the time before. Temmy was only getting what he deserved. He had caused this pain to many, and now he was getting his just reward.

I found the bullet beyond the second knuckle of my index finger. I slid my finger out of the hole and clotted blood came with it.

There was no option. I boiled water and cleansed a handful of cotton cloth, along with my well-used surgical instruments. After some moments, I removed each and set it on the tablecloth next to Temmy. I gave Temmy a warning, and he nodded in understanding.

I pressed the tip of the blade through the skin of his belly and drug the blade southward, opening him up like a gutted fish. Temmy Rowan passed out, which was the best thing that could have happened to him. When the hole was large enough, I reached in and plucked the lead ball from his belly. I used boiled cotton rags to sop up the blood inside and carefully checked to see if the bullet had damaged any internal organs. It had not. I was not careful or gentle with

Temmy Rowan. There was no telling when he would regain consciousness and I wanted to be done before he came to.

Cleaned inside and out, I packed his insides with boiled medicinal herbs, stitched up the wound and then packed the outside of the wound with a wound plaster of herbs. Temmy did not wake for three days.

†††

I found it a pleasure to have intelligent conversation. Not since Maka had I enjoyed a deep conversation with a friend. Yes, I admit that Temmy Rowan became a friend to me as he recovered. He forgot that I was formally possessed by demon spirits, and I forgot that he was a psychopath murderer. We talked about our lives since Bayou de l'Ouest. I communicated to Temmy the reality of our battle with the followers of Adam Thistlewaite, and he leaned into my story, absorbing every nuance of my telling, completely engrossed in the tale.

In turn, he talked of the days following our escape from Bayou de l'Ouest. There was an inquest and a trial in our absence. He said that despite clear evidence of witchcraft, the jury, made up of locals who had been healed by Maka and I, declared our innocence. The city folk who read headlines declared they would rid the land of all witches, and they set out in search of us, but while many pursued, only a few returned. The swamp is a cruel place for the uninitiated.

Rumor had found us in Lake Merchant, but it was a long journey from Cocodrie or Dulac in the belly of the swamps. Once there, the thirst for our heads was forgotten. Over time, I was once again found by those in need of physical or emotional health.

Temmy waxed poetic on the romances he had. He spoke of his search, the conquest, and the relief of their last breath, but it was never in morbid or rough words, always a tender memory. I listened intently, for conversation, even in this brutal form, was welcome to my ear.

A month into his recuperation, I woke in the moonlight to Temmy Rowan, standing over my bed. I could see the look of bloodlust in his eyes through the moonlit window. I could hear his ragged breath as his emotional desire overcame him. In this moment, I knew real fear, for I had neither my baton nor blade with me.

Temmy Rowans strong hands wrapped around my throat and my eyes bulged from the pressure. He crushed my windpipe with the first flex of his hands, then he relaxed and watched as I struggled for breath. These were the moments he lived for. The moments between the initial shock, and the desperate struggle for life. These would be alternated over the next several hours as Temmy played with my life, alternately beating, and strangling me near death. I thought of my parents and of Maka in those hours. I thought of the people I healed and the people I lost. I remembered the faces of those who hunted and hurt me, and those I had killed. As the hours of torture passed, I became less human and more feral. I vacillated between maintaining my life as my own, until death, and calling for my Lwa to rescue me. I knew that if I called to my Lwa, my life would end in different ways, but I could not let Temmy live to harm another woman.

Temmy Rowan would not live to see my death. As I struggled to remain conscious, I called out to my Lwa, and they came with fury. Like lions sprinting towards their prey, Temmy was ripped from me and stapled to the wall of my home. Each of my four Iwa taking hold of an arm or leg as they splayed him like a hide on a barn wall. They could have easily torn him limb from limb, but they wanted my submission. My Iwa had been kept in a limbo for years, and now they demanded my own participation in the bloodletting. In for a penny, in for a pound.

I knew what my call had brought, and I knew how it would end. I swept my feet over the edge of my bed and planted my feet firmly on the floor. I stood on unsteady legs and walked toward Temmy. His face was a mask of insanity, drooling and cackling with sporadic laughter. He knew what was coming, perhaps he always knew. Temmy had killed so many women to witness the moment of death and he had lost his fascination. Now, the only thing that could possibly satisfy Temmy Rowan was to experience death himself. A horrible, painful death. I was prepared to deliver that wish for him.

Drawing from my Lwa, I felt their magic and power fill me. It was erotic and satisfying. It was powerful and compelling. How could I have possibly left this behind? It was the most thrilling experience of my life, and I filled myself with it. I spread my arms wide to take it all in. I threw my head back and laughed with joy, and love, and hate, and anger, all at once.

Before me was a man that I had saved from near death. I had offered him health, food, comfort and even friendship, and he had turned on me. He had betrayed me. Once again, Man had proven that he was a loathsome creature who did not deserve to breath my air, eat my food, or share my comfort.

My Lwa showed me the way. They showed me that together, we could create a new magic, darker and more effective than the old magic. They showed me that my healing magic was a blessing, but my hurting magic was a curse to be used against those who would dare hurt me. With their guidance, I willed my knife to dart across the room and pierce the wound where I had previously removed a bullet from Temmy Rowans belly. The knife sunk to the hilt, forcing the air from Temmy's lungs, and causing a deep, guttural groan to escape his mouth. Through the pain, I could see that this is what Temmy had come for. A ritual death mired in blood, gore, and misery. I stepped to up to him and I promised that I would give him everything he wanted and deserved.

I willed my baton to my fist, and it rushed into the palm of my hand from across the room, solid, secure, ready for work. I brought it down had across his elbow, which shattered under the blow. I swept downward to his knee, laying open the flesh and exposing bone. Wrists, fingers, toes, ear. I struck the most tender and painful parts with my baton. Each blow eliciting a groan of pure ecstasy from Temmy. I did not want him to enjoy this, I wanted him to fear it. He must regret what he had done. I tossed my baton aside and ripped the blade from his belly in an upward slash. I could smell the offal from his intestines as it spilled to the floor. I did not slash or cut, I carved. For over twenty minutes I slowly flayed the skin from his body. After the first, he called out in pleasure. I turned angrily to my spice rack and returned to a small cotton sack of salt. I poured a measure into my hand and then forcefully ground it into the wounds. This gave me the response I wanted. Agony, pain, remorse! Each carve of the knife was followed by a force-ful grinding of coarse salt into the new wound. What was once mewings of pleasure became screams of pain.

Between his cursing and swearing, he repeated over and over, "this is not how you do it! Do it the right way!" But this was the right way. I wished my old cast iron skillet to me, and I poured intense heat into it until it glowed red, waves of heat pouring from the steel. My hand felt no discomfort, but I could smell the charred flesh as I pressed it to the side of Temmy's face. I could taste the acrid smoke in my mouth. Temmy's screams became frantic. Now he was begging for his death. The only thing keeping him alive and awake, was my magic.

In a final act, I picked up my knife by its slippery red handle and plunged it into his heart. His eyes wide, mis mouth moving as if to say, "that's not how you do it". Then he was gone.

My Lwa let Temmy Rowan fall to the floor with a thud. They had demanded my submission by blood and pain, and I had delivered it. As blood dripped from the ceiling into pud-dles on the floor, my Lwa charged into me like a velvet axe. It was not delicate or welcoming, it was a possession, a penalty for leaving them adrift in the spirit world for so many years. Now they were home, and I was theirs forever.

> *What could I do, a woman alone in a world of violence?*
> *What was my choice, to die or be reborn this creature of*
> *sorrow?*
> *What am I now, but a slave to my Lwa?*
> *What of you, who will meet me one day?*

THE SORCIÉRE

Had you been to my domicile in the bayou in the years prior to that day, you would not have recognized the woman I became. The strong, straight woman who had been the savior of so many, became a crooked, bent over crone. My once combed and clean hair once again became matted and oily. My skin broke out in pustules and scars formed over the wounds. My fingers became bent and bony, and I walked with halting steps on my split and bleeding feet. This was my punishment. This was my future. Was it worth it? We shall never know. We hang on to life with such tenacity. In those moments of panic, we would do anything not to die, yet here I was, the living dead. I had traded my very soul for a few more years of life. Little did I know how many years that it would be, for my Lwa fortified my years, even as they tortured my body.

People still came for healing, for the sick are also concerned more with their life than the consequence of an old hag curing them. For the most part, the Lwa allowed me to treat wounds free from their interference, but woe to the man or woman who asked a favor. Beware those who would demand and beg for something beyond mere mortal health, for you will get what you ask for, and you will pay a dear price for the asking.

†††

For many years following, I was once again the witch in the swamps. When you needed me, I granted your wishes, when you did not, you sent your men into the bayou to capture or kill me. Men would come, but they would never leave my meadow. The crocodile, panther and predator ate well and thrived.

Each night, I would plead with my Lwa to let me go, to release me from this servitude, but the price was high, and my flesh would split and bubble, like molten lead. My head would feel like sharp spears were being thrust deep into the skull. They would not release me, and I submitted to their will.

Sometimes I received visitors by the week, other times several in a day, for the world is greedy and desperate for their wants to be realized. They travel by train from the north and East to Dulac, then hire men to transport them down to my domicile, a place all knows of now, but few will come all the way. Now the guides drop their fare off miles away and the path to my door is much longer, winding through the dry land bridges that connect swamp to swamp. They come for a day, but none will stay overnight in the witch's swamp past dusk. Better to sleep in the wilds with the predators than the witch. You are instructed to follow the path, find the witch, make your plea, pay the price, and leave as quickly as possible. This is exactly as I would have it be done, but the Lwa are not so easily pacified. The Lwa are easily bored, and without my dutiful dance and sacrifice, they demand it of those who would come to my door.

I no longer wore the headdress of feathers or smoked the

pungent herbs to bring my Lwa on. I no longer danced and sang for their pleasure, for nothing I did would influence their decisions to heal or harm. I was simply a vessel for them to access this world, and they kept my body captive for this purpose.

It was routine for me to demand to each visitor to gather feathers, moss, and reed to make crude headdresses. They must capture a creature and bleed it over their heads, and they must often take the blade to their arms or legs to bleed themselves. Gossip and rumor had let them know this would be expected and few resisted, assuming correctly that this was the price they must pay for their wish.

The Lwa would delight in this self-harm. It was so much more exciting than when Maka and I simply danced and sang. These people would hurt *themselves* in devotion and worship of the Lwa. On occasion, an Lwa would abandon my body to possess the visitor. In these moments, I felt both emptiness and relief, as it often happens with the prisoner. I was indeed a prisoner of these Lwa. I was not a willing host, but I was the host, nonetheless. Serving both man and spirit.

Back in the cities, I was spoken of as a parlor trick, a miraculous, fantastic side-show that must be experienced. The more people came, the more the Lwa were fed and the more the people of Dulac and Cocodrie profited from the tourism. My legend grew. Plays were written about me, and I was the source of endless stories in the saloons and by the campfire. The witch of the swamp. The demon from hell. Yet I was as empty as a dry well. I was listless, lifeless and without feeling.

Numb as the stump of a limb that has been hacked off, but never completely void of feeling.

No more did the people send their heroes to slay the witch. They sent in reporters and playwrights to learn my story. In my silence, they made up fantastic creations of who I was, and my bond with the Devil himself.

I tried to leave, but the Lwa would not allow it, for they were center stage and loving the attention. I tried to resist the spectators, but the Lwa thrust me back into their limelight. I was a trained seal, performing tricks for the masses, who never realized I was not a witch at all, but the instrument of spirits who had possessed me. I was a captive.

Once, a commander of the Confederate Army of the South came with a small platoon of men to request my audience with Mr. Jackson, the leader of their movement. I communicated that I would not leave our bayou home, but that Mr. Jackson was welcome to visit us. The negotiation became more intense as the request became a demand, and then force.

The Lwa were elated at this opportunity to wrack havoc on so many at one time. I felt the cool rush of wind as the Lwa fled my body to assault the platoon. Instantly I turned and ran on pained legs as quickly as I could, but the Lwa would not be abandoned again. They blinded the men and stole their eyes, then returned, circling me in dance with their newfound toys. One by one, they entered my soul, as gently as could be. There was no more force and violence in them, only happiness and excitement. Not even my attempt to flee could dampen their mood.

Under the confident leadership of the commander, a few of the patrol felt their way back up the path on hand and knee, hours later coming to the docks to the surprise of their boatmen. My Lwa had won the battle, but the war would be much different.

CAPTURE

The return of the blinded patrol had been a tactical bless-ing for the South, which was at risk of losing the war. With this witch a potential new weapon, they could turn the tides and perhaps even win. Generals met in smoky rooms to dis-cuss how to coax or capture the me, and how to use me to their advantage if they could.

The fighting had been fierce, and the Confederate Army was being pushed further back into the Southern Territory. They needed a miracle to save their cause, and this witch from the swamp was a last straw effort.

Armed with the gossip, musings, stories, and assumptions of hundreds of interviews, fifty-six soldiers walked out of the bayou and spread out across my meadow. On creeping soles of well-polished boots, they quietly made their way up the meadow slope to my domicile in the pre-dawn hours of morn-ing. They caught me sleeping, and within that, the Lwa were not alerted to the danger. Even as I awoke to a soldier standing over me, I did not fret, for I was as calm as a gentle breeze thorough the tall grass of the glades. I was at utter peace and calm, attempting to keep my Lwa resting.

The soldiers quietly bound me in strong rope, careful not

to hurt me, and they lifted me on their shoulders for the trek back to their boats. I would remain placid and calm all the way to Savannah, my Lwa oblivious to the situation at hand.

Still bound, I was carried to the commanders briefing room, where bearded men of stout girth and advancing years wore the grey of the Confederacy. The commander himself addressed me with respect and kindness, although I could see from the look on his face that he was revolted by my sight.

He spoke of the cause and the need, and made his request, like so many men before him. I looked through empty eyes as he made his plea. He switched tactics and ordered my binds undone. He ordered womenfolk to draw a bath for me, and to gather clean clothing. It would take several draining's of filthy water before I was clean, and the clothes hung from my atrophied body like sackcloth, but it was the first time I had felt human in many years, still I did not wake my Lwa.

I was again brought before the commander and his gathered officers. This time I told them, as best as possible, my situation. I told them that it was not me, but the spirits that enslaved me that caused the miracles. I made it clear that I was simply a vessel for these Spirits, and that only they could help or hurt the Southern cause. I communicated that once I woke the spirits, there was no telling what they would do, or how they would react.

I was excused while the soldiers discussed at length the situation before them. It was determined that men loyal to the cause should take in these spirits, drawing them out of me, and into the service of the Confederacy. Doubtful, but desperately optimistic, I prepared an ounfò in a service tent, preparing all the things that four strong men would need to entice and accept the Lwa into them. I instructed the volunteers in the rituals, and I taught them how to capture the Lwa within their spirits.

When all was prepared, the men smoked the sacred herb and began to dance and chant as I had taught them. It did not take long to wake the Lwa, for they were well rested and full of vitality and energy. So long they had waited for a proper ritual. Here were four willing men. Each strong of body and heart. Each willingly offering themselves to the Lwa. And the Lwa joined with the men, possessing each one as they celebrated their great success with more song and dance. And while the Lwa were drunk with pleasure, I walked out of the tent and into a waiting carriage. I had honored my end of the bargain, and now the commander would honor his. The driver struck the horse with the whip, and we launched off into the night, headed for Dulac.

†††

The following morning, the men woke to tight throats and aching heads. The Lwa had found themselves without their favored host, and each was entombed in a new body and mind. Bodies and minds that they did not know or understand. These men had not given up the entirety of their selves to the Lwa over many years. They did not feel the same or act the same. They were confident where I was broken. They had a mission where I had only subservience. They had demands to make of the Lwa where I had been an empty vessel.

Perhaps most disturbing was that they had spent so many years in a single body and mind, and now they were separated.

They felt disoriented and adrift. Spirits like to be anchored to a host, not held by tenuous strings. Upon waking, the Lwa were restless and on the edge of anger. Each host tried to calm their respective Lwa. They spoke of the great privilege to be serving the confederacy, of the cause and the need to win. Each man felt that they were losing control of their Lwa, and they began to dance and chant once again, pacifying the Lwa with praise and adulation. This is the weakness of every spirit. The praise of man. The gift of dance and song. All that was missing was the sacrifice. Hesitantly, the men went to the prison where the Union prisoners were kept. They gave order to bind four prisoners and deliver them to a remote part of the encampment. Repulsed and mortified, the men were helpless as the Lwa controlled minds and spirits to draw their daggers across arm and leg of the prisoners. The screaming was heard across the camp, and chilled everyone to the bone, but this was how they would win the war, and it must be done. As officers trembled in their comfortable houses, men were being bled to death slowly within earshot. The sacrifice was a great joy to the Lwa, who would demand this ritual be replayed over and again as the campaign wore on.

The day would come when the possessed men would be taken to the front lines to engage the Lwa with the enemy. The first day was a slaughter, with the Lwa slaying tens of Union soldiers in glorious bloodlust. This was followed by an evening of dance and song, filling the Lwa with absolute pleasure.

The second day found a new wave of Union solders dying spectacular deaths, then the third, fourth and fifth repeating. The Confederate commanders were elated. The troop moral was high, but things were not as cozy for the Lwa and their hosts. The men were drained and exhausted. They had endured five straight days and nights of slaughter and celebration. They were dead on their feet while the Lwa were demanding more slaughter, more song, and more dance. They were drunk with power and lust. They were in a frenzy state and could not come down. Each day that followed there was more death, but less celebration. The song and dance had ceased. They were now simple killing machines. It was no longer fun and exciting; it had become monotonous and demanding. As one, the Lwa realized that the humans had lured them into doing their dirty work. They were now slaves to humanity. Enraged, the Lwa turned on the Confederacy, wiping out the entirety of the garrison in within two bloody days. No man, woman or child was left breathing. The men who hosted the Lwa were completely broken. Their minds a scattered mush. They had seen and done this to their own people, under complete control of the Lwa. They were supposed to be the saviors, instead they were the death of the cause.

†††

Four men in tattered and bloody Confederate grey walked the miles across Georgia, Alabama, and Mississippi. They passed through the cities of Biloxi, Slidell, and Baton Rouge before turning South to Houma, Dulac and Cocodrie. Emaciated and near death, they hired a man to pole them by pirogue into the Bayou. By the time they reached my meadow, they were near death from the march.

It was here that they sat on the ground beyond my porch,

waiting for me to help them. It was here, in my meadow that I negotiated with the Lwa. They needed me and I did not need them. They could take me by force but knew that I would leave them at first opportunity once again. I knew I could never escape them on my own, and so the need for a formal negotiation. I had demands, which were resolute and firm. They had needs, which were selfish and self-serving.

We talked for three days. I fed the men and demanded the Lwa restore their health. The Lwa had no concern for the welfare of man, only for their own. Still, they complied and each man slowly regained strength and vitality. Each day we met in the meadow to discuss our options, and to determine a course that we could all live with.

The final decisions were made, and I allowed my original Lwa to possess me once again, although now on my terms. No longer would it lord over and rule me. We would coexist together, sharing our gifts and working together.

The remaining three Lwa would be free to roam the living world, seeking adherents of Vodou who would welcome them, but they were no longer welcome inside me.

In agreement, the four men would be free to keep or reject the Lwa that possessed them. All had lived through a terrible hell of death followed by the forced march back to the Bayou. None wanted to be possessed any longer, and they were released from their Lwa, who simply stepped out of their soul, and stood before me in the waning of daylight.

Standing tall and respectful, my Lwa stepped into my soul, but it was unlike other times. He was grateful for my acceptance, and in turn, I showed him the respect and hospitality that would cement our new relationship.

As the three Lwa left the men, I felt a pang of guilt for the Lwa who had been Maka's. I was losing the last piece of Maka, my greatest friend. I was also losing those pieces of my parents through their Lwa. On reflection, they were neither Maka or my parents, they were unwelcome parasites that had latched onto those I loved, and I was grateful that they would now be gone. Still, I respectfully acknowledged the Lwa as they left my meadow in search of the spirit world.

I tried to remain in the Bayou, but the stories followed me there. Once again, I was beset by the greedy, the needy and the demanding. Southern Confederate sympathizers hunted us, and the families of Northern Unionists wanted to avenge the deaths of their families. Although I was safe in this hostile place where others were unfamiliar, it no longer felt like home.

The day came when I left our domicile in the Bayou. We left by pirogue, poling West to Raccourci Bay, then northwest to Jug Lake, poling down the large tributary bayou and emerging from the comfort and familiarity of the swamp into the massive Fourleage bay. So large was the bay, I could not see the opposite shore on the clearest day, but I knew it was hours to the South. I crafted oars from saplings on the shore and I rowed West for two weeks, finally reaching Big Carencro Bayou. I crossed over, staying on the Fourleague for three more weeks until I made Halters Island, a place of pirates and criminals. I provisioned using some of the gold I had hoarded over many years of barter, but I used it sparingly, and only as a last resort. I was an old hag, and not a target for those looking for an easy rape, but I was a target for an easy coin. I kept my head low while my Lwa stayed on guard, and we passed through Halter's without incident.

I navigated Halters by way of the Creole pass, a bayou that connected the Fourleague with the Atchafalaya Bay, a predecessor to the Gulf of Mexico. It was stormy and rugged. The coastlines offered many places to come ashore, but few that were inhabited. I made for the Atchafalaya River where I sold my pirogue at Plumb Island, and boarded a steamer heading north, inland to Morgan City. It was there that I slept in my first store-bought bed since my youth in Cocodrie. I stayed three days in Morgan City. I bathed, had my hair cropped close to the head to rid it of the tangles, snarls and lice that had been the state for so long. I purchased new clothing of the region, including a fashionable hat. The women in the store had to show me how to dress, for this was all new to me. Even the confederate clothing had not been this complicated and uncomfortable, but I did not want to attract attention.

In my new attire, I was nearly invisible. I was simply an old lady traveler, headed west. I purchased coach passage to San Antonio, and settled in for a long, dusty ride out of Louisiana and into the western frontier.

The destination was predictable. Baton Rouge to Lafayette, then to Lake Charles, Beaumont and to the bustling City of Houston, but this was still too close. I needed distance between myself and the rumors that followed me. I arrived in San Antonio in the late afternoon. I was hot and tired, but not the same heat as the swamps. This was dry heat, blistering and beautiful. There were no mosquitos or chiggers to gnaw on my hide. The layers of clothing were stifling, but it was entirely bearable.

I stepped from the stage on stiff legs, assisted by the coach driver, who had been a gentleman the entire trip. He helped me to a local hotel, where I checked in and washed up before returning to the lobby in search of a meal. My gold was quickly whittling down, and I was thrifty with my few remaining coins. A few pennies for dinner and another penny for tea. I sat in the picture window of the café, watching the bustle of a booming western town. Men wore tall hats, and the ladies wore voluminous dresses. Everyone was as dusty as the roads but seemed to be immune to its filth. A few men wore guns at their waists, but fewer than I had heard about. In all, it seemed a civilized place to live. Perhaps I could stay a while and work to build a stake before moving on? But my Lwa was wiser and more suspect of humanity. He urged me to move on, and we did.

I bought passage on the stagecoach headed further west, but we made it only a few days drive to Boerne. I stepped off the coach on the shores of Cibolo Creek, while the driver watered the horses. I felt a peace I had not known since my childhood. My Lwa felt it in me, and he offered that we could stay and travel the area for a day or two. The only lodging was a small house that let a room to travelers. The bed was ridden with mice, but otherwise clean enough. I had certainly shared my bed with worse. We rented a buckboard and two horses to pull it, and the man of the house pointed us towards Sisterdale, a hamlet of a half dozen settlers surrounded by miles of ranchland.

It took a full day to reach the village, where we were greeted by the locals with fanfare. Travelers rarely came to this area, and they wanted to hear stories of who I was and where I had been.

A community dinner was quickly planned, and a dozen folks and a few kids came together to break bread and visit. It was entirely unexpected and delightful. Questions came from every corner of the room, and people shouted out guesses before I could respond. When they learned I was a healer, they mistook that for "Doctor", and they began telling me of all the wonderful places and experiences to be had if I were to choose to join their community. The nearest Doctor was in Boerne, and they would welcome a doctor in their own small town. To all the surrounding ranches and communities, it would be a tremendous boon. I would agree to stay a few days to look at the land, and a great cheer went up from the assembled, bringing a rare smile to my wrinkled and aged old face.

There was much laughter and comradery before a fiddle was brought out and we danced the evening into twilight. My Lwa was elated. Dancing among new friends, the playing of music, and none of it had the strings of obligation of demand attached to it. It was purely for the joy of celebration. I could feel my Lwa embrace these people, and I did as well.

I moved into a small, abandoned bunkhouse near the Guadalupe creek. It was close enough to the other houses that I was enveloped in the safety of the community, but far enough away for the privacy I needed to set up the ounfò, and practice my Vodou, for the Lwa required this as his own negotiation. Together, we established a small medical clinic on the range, working together to support our new friends, and those that were to come. All was well with our small world.

†††

It was not enough that the ladies of the Sisterdale came to scrub my bunkhouse clean before I moved in, the menfolk brought gifts of furniture, a bed with a horsehair mattress and a pantry full of food.

Over the next few weeks, the assembled built a small surgery adjoining the house, and a low-walled outdoor hospital like the one we had in Cocodrie. I had brought scarce herbs and medicines with me on this journey, and I knew little of the medicinal value of the local flora. The best way to learn was to speak with the natives who lived in and around the community. For weeks, I traveled by my buckboard from home to home, introducing myself to the local native American peoples, and learning who held the knowledge of local medicinal plants and herbs. Where the swamp is chock-a-buck full of plants of every variety, the dry desert environment was sparse and seemingly void of life. Still, everyplace on the earth will take care of man and animal if you know what to look for and how to prepare it. Thousands of years of knowledge passed down through those who will listen. Although much knowledge had been lost since the great Indian wars, there was still much for me to learn. Soon I had a house-full of drying herbs, and the local men built a patio surrounding the bunkhouse where I could dry the herbs under cover. When a traveler needed to know where the doctor lived, they were told to look for the house covered in dried plants.

And come they did. Snake-bites, whooping cough, broken

bones, and broken hearts. People seemed to like talking to me and would bare their soul without interruption or condescension. I listened while I worked, and quickly became known throughout the region as a capable, if not brilliant doctor. Still, I was conservative with the power I held. I say power because my Lwa and I had become somewhat of a partnership in our work. Healing is more than sewing up a wound or dispensing an herb. Confidence in the doctor, and the doctor's confidence in their treatment, inspires healing. Timing of treatments, knowing when to move forward and when to wait it out. There is also a magical component to all healing. It is not luck, it is belief, inspired by true magic that can turn the worst-case scenario into a survivable cure. With or without my Lwa, this magic occurs in nature, but with my Lwa, I was able to heal when others would have given up. Together, we were a powerful healing force, and our community, and the neighboring ranches were the beneficiaries of this magic.

I am compelled to relate the story of Major Dunstill, Union Army, retired. He had founded a small ranch on the Guadalupe with hard work and the support of local neighbors. He had helped me move into my home and had assisted with the building of the hospital. He was a leader of this community and well loved by all.

When the Major had not returned to his ranch at an expected time, several ranch hands spread out in search of him. By the next day, the search had expanded to our entire community, and within days all the ranches in the area were searching for Major Dunstill.

He was found at the bottom of a canyon. His horse lay

dead nearby. It was clear from the scene that he and his horse had fallen from the cliff some thirty foot above, perhaps during a nighttime ride.

Men fished his body from the ravine and brought him to my hospital by wagon, arriving long after midnight. I had lanterns lit in the surgery, and my tools and likely herbs at the ready. Water was boiling on the potbelly stove, and we had an assortment of rags in the hot water, ready for dressing.

Men lay the Major on the surgical table, which was no more than a pine slab on sawhorses and stepped back into the shadows to watch with the women. I quickly shooed them outside, but removing the women was a harder task, each thinking that I could not possibly work alone. But I needed to. I cut off his boots and trousers and peeled back the shirt to see what damage had been done. I could hear the wheezing of his ragged breath and knew that he likely punctured a lung before I peeled back his shirt. Ribs on both sides were bruised or broken, but it was obvious that he had taken a serious blow to his left side and a rib had indeed pierced his lung. A quick examination of the rest of the body concluded that this was the most urgent wound, and my Lwa and I began to work.

I gathered up several reeds harvested from the Guadalupe and tossed them into the boiling water for just 30 seconds. This was a crude but capable attempt of sterilization for the time. Using my blade, I cut a small incision between the ribs that had been broken. First, I stuck my finger into the incision, curved it at the knuckle and lifted the broken rib back into place. Although I had done this many times, I was always grateful when the patient was unconscious, as the Major was.

This would likely have been excruciating if he were awake. As I lifted, my Lwa was healing the bone in place. It was a tentative tack at best, but it kept the bone from separating again. With my finger, I probed inside the cut, looking for the puncture in the lung. Having found it, I took one of the hollow reeds and slipped it into the incision, and into the hole in the lung. This would allow the fluid to drain. I stitched around my incision with catgut and a needle, and then turned the major on his side so that the tube would drain the accumulated fluid in the lung. It dripped out slowly, but nearly an ounce came out before it stopped.

Again, I felt the flow of magic from my Lwa as he sought to coax the fluid out, and to heal the wound. Next was to set the broken bone in his femur and the two broken bones in his left arm. Last, we used a straight razor to shave his hair away from the gash in his scalp, and we stitched up the wound and patched it with a plaster. We drained the last of the lung and lay the Major on his back. Calling in two men, they assisted me in wrapping the Majors torso tightly in bandages. Four hours had passed, and I was all-out. Buoyed by the loving embrace of my Lwa, I washed my face in the porcelain basin, and lay on my pallet-bed, asleep in moments.

I slept through the morning, and the townspeople, although in my yard awaiting news, did not wake me. They had seen the lamp turned down in my home in the early hours of morning, and knew I needed sleep. Along late afternoon, I could smell coffee brewing, and beefsteaks on a grill. Famished, I rose from my bed, and checked on the Major. His breathing was steady, if not slightly labored, but the work looked good, and his chances were better than when he had arrived. I quickly washed and threw on a fresh dress, for I owned several by now and loved the smell of freshly laundered clothing that had dried in the sun.

Stepping out onto my porch, I could see the assembly of a half dozen folk sitting next to a fire-ring, cooking an evening meal. They turned to me, and I offered a heartfelt appreciation for their care and concern. I shared that the Major was quite ill, but he had a fighting chance, and the rest was up to him. The assembled welcomed me forward and poured me a cup of strong coffee, which I had learned to enjoy, and cut a generous slab of beef. They added two drop-biscuits with a slab of fresh-churned butter, and I was soon tucking in to my meal like a woman half-starved.

Major Dunston was an old man, and slow to heal. I had him moved to my pallet, and I slept on the floor, to the displeasure of the locals. As he rested, they added on another room to my home. A room for recovering guests. They made a new pallet bed and when it was done, I found it so pleasant I opted to use this room myself.

They days passed, and the Major recovered. He watched as I treated men and children. He saw me take the coin of those who could pay, trade with those who could not, and my charity of those who had nothing. He never spoke to me, other than to say please or thank you. He watched and wondered.

Major Dunston was not an ignorant man. Years of fighting the confederate enemy had taught him to be observant, and wary. He knew the ways of the field surgery because he had carried three bullets and a blade over his years of campaigning.

He knew how the educated doctor operated his surgery and consulted his library of medical books. None of these were evident in my healing. Where the Doctor is a medical academic, I was raised in a practical application of healing. I worked with the tools I had at hand, often improvising.

Major Dunston knew I was an old woman, but he could not tell the number of years I had lived. He would not have believed that in this year of 1882, I was already ninety-one years to his sixty. My hair had returned and was brushed daily, pulled into a grey knot at the back of my head, as was the fashion of the day. My neck was creased with wrinkles, but still long and lithe, a few tendrils of hair loose down my back. My hands were calloused and blotched with scar and stain, but they were strong and nimble. But it was my eyes that held his attention. My eyes were as aware and awake as a young woman. They were the eyes of a woman who had known fear and strength. One who had vast experience, and the confidence that comes with it. He also saw that I was unafraid of any man or Indian. He had seen this strength in the strongest, most capable men. It was as if I knew nothing, or no one could harm me. But I knew something he did not. I knew my Lwa would protect me against any danger. In this knowledge I was at peace.

The Major would eventually sit up in his bed, with assistance, then came the day he took a few steps to the porch and collapsed into a bentwood rocker, gasping for breath. It was here he muttered something about getting old and weak. I told him that age was earned, and to not complain about the pains and aches that came with it. He smiled for the first time since I knew him, and we sat together on the porch sipping coffee, watching the wind move the tall grass like water. This place was so unlike my swamps that were enclosed by thick cypress and undergrowth. Take ten steps off the path and you could lose your way. This made hiding as easy as slipping into the dense undergrowth. But here, in Texas, you could see for miles. I could see anyone coming long before they arrived, but I had nowhere to hide.

These were bucolic and relaxing days, the first I had known since childhood. My Lwa seemed to have aged with me, no longer longing for bloodlust. No longer vain and needy. My peace seemed to flow through my Lwa, and we coexisted in a mildly tense harmony, the same way an old married couple would. We would never both be perfectly content at the same time, but this was as close as we would likely get.

And Major Dunston recovered, albeit with a limp requiring a cane. Long after he could have gone home, he stayed on, fetching water from the well, driving the wagon to far-flung herb harvesting places, and generally being a generous helpmate. Unless I was working with a patient, we spent each morning and evening sitting on the porch, quietly rocking. Although he was unlike Maka in every way possible, he filled the void that Maka had left. We had no apparent intimacy, yet we shared a closeness of spirit that we both appreciated. We both felt the need for companionship, but neither needed more.

The Major, as noted, was an observant man. It took no time at all for him to recognize the moments I would steal away from the makeshift hospital and retire to the small outbuilding where I had made a small ounfó. He would notice the glazed look on my face when I returned, and he could smell the acrid smoke on my dress. Sometimes there would be a small spatter of blood on my shoes or dress from my offering, for I kept a coop of chickens and turkeys, and often captured lizards, snakes, and mice about the property, much to his amusement.

Recognizing his curiosity, and after some time had passed, I shared a small piece of my work with the Major. A taste to quell his curious thirst, but not enough to rouse suspicion. Sitting on the porch as the dusk crept over the landscape, I sat my chair directly in front of his own and began to speak. As always, he sat quietly as I told him of my gift of healing, as given by my parents, and my gift of magic, as given by Maka. I shared that this magic was not born of parlor tricks or sleight of hand, but of a benevolent spirit that dwelled inside of me. This spirit amplified my existing knowledge and care, allowing me to heal when others could not.

Major Dunston sat thoughtful for long moments before speaking. I have heard of such things, he said, but have no personal knowledge other than the miraculous healing you performed for me. "I ask you now if you are a prisoner to this spirit, of if it dwells within you of your free will?"

I said my Lwa spirit was welcome into me, and that it was both protector and assist to my work.

Major Dunston asked if my spirit was aware of our conversation, and I replied that it was. He drew his pipe from his breast pocket and spent moments packing it with tobacco, then lighting it. A lazy tendril of smoke rose from the pipe and a great billow of smoke from his mouth before he spoke.

"Please share with your spirit that I am grateful for its healing of me, and its protection of you. I have grown fond of you, and if you, and your spirit, would accept me into your small family, I would also protect you, and your spirit to my dying breathe."

I cannot remember the last time my heart overflowed with love, happiness, and gratitude. I had lived with so much rejection, threat, and pain, that to have anyone speak these words to me was a poultice on my soul. I felt the same from my Lwa, for it knew the heart of this man, and knew it was true.

For many years we lived together in a harmonious home. We shared every part of ourselves but our bodies, for he was too old for such things, and I had never truly known a man. We were content with what we shared and basked in the happiness that it contained.

ON THE RUN

The years spent with the major were remarkable. Never did he ask more about my Lwa, never would I share more. There was an acceptance. He grew older and more fail, and I grew older and stronger. Still, he was an exceptional helpmate and we worked together to heal those who came to our door.

But no good deed goes unpunished. My reputation preceded me, as always. What was once a few locals who came to my hospital for help, became a steady stream from San Antonio, Dallas, Houston, and other far-reaching places. Still, I did not worry, for I was a new woman, reborn, and with an entirely different life and reputation.

But still they came. From the western towns of Tucson, the northern towns of Colorado, up from the Mexican border, and eventually, from as far East as the Carolinas.

It was the woman from New York that caused alarm. She pulled up in front of the hospital in a surrey-coach pulled by matching bay horses, I felt my skin crawl. My Lwa had warned me that evil was coming to our door, and I was helpless to deter it. The Major, immaculately dressed, clean shaved, and managing the steps with the assistance of his ivory-tipped cane, went to the coach to greet our guest. He offered his hand

and led her down the stair. Her highly polished city shoes immediately covered in a layer of white dust. Her hair was piled high atop her head and crowned with a purple velvet hat and white lace veil. Her clothing was extraordinary, and expensive, with layers of blouses beneath the heavy velvet drape. She walked confident and steady across the uneven ground on her low, black heels. She was practiced and perfect. Cultured and manicured.

The major again offered his hand and escorted her up the steps to the porch, and then inside, where I had hidden from sight. I quickly escaped into the back room, considering how to avoid the inevitable. While the Major poured her a tall glass of spring water from our well, I sat frozen, waiting for the moment I knew would come.

The Major inquired of the woman her reason for visiting the hospital, for she looked to be in fine health. She did not beat about the bush or play coy. She simply said, "I have come for the Witch".

"There is no Witch here" replied the major with a hint of laughter, "could you be more specific"?

"I have need of your Witch and I will see her now please", said the women with curt annoyance. The Major excused himself and came into my room, closing the door behind him. He stood for a moment on weak legs, observing my fear. He intuitively knew that this person was a danger to me. He also saw in me something else. It was the full power of my Lwa, bristling and glowing about me. I could feel it's tension as it writhed and stewed in my soul. I did not know whether it was fearing for my safety, or lusting for prey, for it had been years since it had been turned loose on one who would make demands on it. The Major simply nodded his head and left the room to rejoin the woman.

He approached the woman as she sipped the cool water and apologized for her long travel, but that perhaps it would be best if she left. There was no Witch here, and she had made the trip in vain.

The woman stood slowly, towering over the Majors stooped and failing body. Her impatience was evident, and she did not ask permission, but side-stepped him and burst into my room without a knock or announcement. I stood at the far end of the small room, straight as a stick, as powerful as my Lwa could make me. I was not just commanding, I was powerful, and the woman was stopped in her tracks, as did the Major, who entered behind the woman. Both had expected to see this stooped and frail crone. An old woman, but the visage before them was awesome and fearful.

The woman's confidence and bearing dropped immediately. For the first time in many years, she knew real fear, and it was standing in front of her. Like a bear or a panther that is cornered, I bared my teeth and hissed a snarl from my throat.

The woman recognized her folly, and slowly bowed before me, not daring to look down, but fearing to look in my eyes. She stared at my chin and apologized for her rude interruption. Her previously pristine countenance was now covered in a layer of sweat, as if the heat in the room had increased by degrees. Major Dunston stood quiet. He knew real fear of battle, when a man is cornered and has no choice but to fight for his life. He knew the danger that I was in, but he also knew the danger I embodied.

With a nod, I dismissed the Major, and he hesitantly left the room, closing the door behind him. I knew he remained just beyond, listening, for he had sworn his protection, but it was obvious that I had control over this situation.

With tension wrapped in grace, I motioned for the woman to stand. Her knees knocked together as she stood on unsteady legs.

I told her that I had left that life behind. That I had a new life that was good and peaceful, and that she had torn that peace asunder. With intensity, I demanded she leave, and never speak of me again.

She stood stock-still for a moment, looking at the wooden plank floor and the edge of the rag-wound rug. She found a little iron for her spine and straightened, only then daring to look at me. Once the words started, I could not have stopped them, for it was a mad rush.

"I have followed the bits and pieces of your trail over the years to find you. I have had so many failures, and met so many women, none were you. Forgive me if I have hardened to the task, but I never expected to find you when I arrived here. I assumed another fruitless end, but I have found you, and it is so very important that you hear me out."

My Lwa was coiled as if to spring, but I calmed it, softening just a little. "Come outside, I told her, you are not welcome in my home, but I will hear you outside."

She opened the door and there stood the Major, a pistol in his hand, and a look of readiness on his face. I could not have loved him more in this moment. Together, we followed her out of the dim light of the house into the full sunshine of the day. Both the Major and I circled her to get the sun out of our eyes and into hers. He knew this trick from years of battle, and I guess I knew it for the same reason.

Shielding her eyes, she stated that she was Andra Simmon's, a writer for the New York Tribune. She had been writing about the folk tales and legends of America and had become fixated on my own story. While most were tall tales, the stories of the Swamp Witch of Louisiana had a haunting realism. The witnesses were terrified, and despite great incentive to do so, would not lead Miss Simmons into the swamps. She had pieced together the stories of the spirits, of Maka and even traced his own lineage back to Saint-Domingue. The stories she published in the Tribune were favorites of her readers. *Tales that would peel the skin off your ears*, they would say. She noted that the word *Witch* had become too common and had lost its edge. Along the way, she had adopted a pen name rooted in the French, and perhaps even French-Cajun word for witch, the *Sorcière*. A sorceress. She closed her fast-running explanation with an expression of respect and apology. "I know why you left Louisiana. I know that you are not looking for celebrity or fame. I know you want your peace and solitude, and I hope you have found it here. My readers are engrossed in this story, they are passionate about it. I would like to give them closure by letting them know what has become of you. Please, will you speak with me?"

It was a strange feeling in that moment. For as absolute that I was in rejection of this request, I could feel my Lwa leaning in, wanting me to continue this discussion. But my Lwa was not reflecting trust or comfort, it was thinking about all the people that would come because of such a story. My Lwa had sat dormant for years, and this visit had made its blood boil. It wanted dancing, song, and blood.

I did not care what the Major thought in this moment. My decision was my own. I took the woman by the elbow and forcefully walked her to her carriage. When she resisted, I all but threw her up into the seat, amazed at my own strength in my advanced years.

You will leave, you will never speak of this day for the rest of your life. You may tell your reader any story you care to of Louisiana and the swamps, but should a single soul seek me out here, I will hunt you down and you will learn of spirits and death. I slapped the rump of the horse nearest to me and they took off like a shot, nearly spilling Miss Simmons out of the carriage. The dust flew from the wheels as she regained control and sped down the lane, back to who knows where. It could have ended there, but at a distance she stopped and turned her carriage around to face us. Even at this distance I could see the rage and resolve in her face. She turned the carriage back down the lane and disappeared into the distance, leaving only a cloud of dust in her wake.

†††

The Major waited for my explanation, but I had no words. I began sobbing, with my entire body rising and falling with my labored breath. He wrapped his arms around me and held me for long minutes as my tears soaked through his rough denim shirt. When I had cried my last tear, I straightened up and went inside the house to prepare dinner.

It was a light meal of roasted chicken and herbs that grew about the yard. We split an ear of corn gifted to me by a patient the day prior, and the sweet, firm kernels burst with flavor in each bite. I had not enjoyed this curious vegetable since Maka and I arrived in Cocodrie, I had become quite fond it here in Texas. We washed it down with the juice of pomegranates that grew wild in the foothills, strained in an old cotton dishtowel which had become the most beautiful crimson thereafter.

We cleared the table and washed up together, a ritual since our early days. We then retired to the porch, each to their own rocker, and we listened to the stillness of the Texas night.

After a time, I stood to face him. We must leave, I said. He gave me a curious look and bade me to continue my explanation. And so, I told him my tale. The story of Maka, and of magic, and treachery and murder. When it became too dark to see, I lit an oil lamp and continued deep into the night. For so long I had kept these secrets, and now they flooded out of me. I ended my tale when they had brought him to my dinner table, lay him out and I healed him with the help of my Lwa.

He rose from the chair and held me tight, wrapping me in his warm embrace. He led me into the house, and we shared a bed together for the first time.

We woke tangled in each other, and we both smiled in a bashful and innocent way. He rose first and left the room, giving me my privacy to dress. When I stepped out into the main room, coffee was on the stove and thick slabs of bacon were spitting in an old cast-iron skillet. There was no sign of the Major and I rightly assumed he had gone to collect eggs, for he returned shortly with six medium sized brown eggs. He broke them into the bacon grease, and we watched together as the sputtered and spit, cooking in the hot oil. He bade me to the table and poured me a cup of strong black coffee, then fetched two dishes from the cupboard and fished the bacon and eggs out of the skillet with a wooden spatula I had made the year prior.

The coffee was strong, and the eggs runny, the bacon the perfect amount of crisp at the edges, but still chewy. Like every morning, the only sound was our wooden spoons scraping the last of the yolk from our crockery plates, and the satisfied creak of our old wooden chairs. For anyone in the modern world who had not enjoyed the absolute peace and quiet of the morning without the need to speak, or be heard, I highly recommend it.

Before we cleared the table, the Major leaned his forearms on the heavy wooden table and leaned in. The very same table I had healed him on so many years before. A table stained with the blood of a hundred patients, a thousand chickens and tens of thousands of cups of spilled coffee. It was an old friend, stained with good memories.

I knew who you were from the moment you started healing in our village, he said. I have heard the tales of your magic and witchery over the years during my travels through Louisiana and the South. There is speculation that you are conjuring spirits to aid in your witchery. Like many, I was fascinated, if not a bit repulsed, for we weak humans are often drawn to that which we do not understand and cannot explain. I followed the stories told in small café's, churches and even men's barber shops. It seems that for years, the most interesting stories were about the Witch of the Swamps.

The New York newspapers began to write about you. The stories were riveting, if not inflated and macabre for the sake of drama. I read these stories on every occasion, as riveted to them as thousands of other readers.

And then you came to our small corner of the world. You fit every description, but better dressed and less evil than portrayed. I watched closely in the early days, looking for signs of your sorcery and witchcraft, but you hid it well. Only by being observant could I see your change before healing. I secretly inspected the small shed where you worship. I spied on you while you were possessed. During this entire time, I was not repulsed or afraid, I was admiring of your commitment to those you cared for. I was touched by the symbiotic nature of you and your Lwa. I was grateful for your healing of me, and I was falling in love with the woman you are and have been. Nothing in this world could keep me from protecting you, as you have protected me. I am bound to you, both in devotion, and in our secret.

I sat still as a stone, unsure what to say, or how to act. Urged by my Lwa, I threw my arms around his neck and held on for dear life, afraid he would run, grateful he did not.

We held each other for long minutes before he pulled away and looked with compassionate resolve in his eyes. We need to leave, he said quietly, almost reverently. She will write and they will come for you. You will have no rest or peace, for the greedy will hunt you out, and the vigilante will hunt you down. She was the first, but she will not be the last.

Without a word, he walked out of the house and fetched our two horses from the corral. He hitched them to the wagon while I hastily packaged the things we would need and that which we could not live without. I had come to Texas with nothing but an extra change of clothing and a few medical instruments. I was leaving with a crate of herbs, a crate of medical tools, a crate of kitchen essentials, a crate of blankets and bedding, and the Major and I split a crate for clothing and boots.

The year was 1892. The Major was seventy years old, and although he thought me in my seventies, I would soon be one-hundred and two. He was still capable, but he moved with the age that told a story of his years, his battles, and his wounds. As I watched him heave the last of the crates into the back of the wagon, I realized that he would not be with me long, and that I would once again be alone.

HAVANA

Rather than travel through Boerne, we cut across old ranch roads to Kendalia, then south to San Antonio. Over the years, this large town had become a small city. Some of the roads within the town were built of cobbled stones, making the journey much more comfortable than the uneven dirt roads we traversed over many miles. Along the way, the Major talked, and I listened. He had considered our quandary through the night and determined that if we stayed in America, I would be hunted. He had spent months in Cuba as a young man, while in the merchant marine. This was an old civilization, one that understood the old ways. It was close enough to Saint-Domingue to have adherents of Vodou, far enough away to prevent radical interference and influence.

As he spoke, my Lwa listened intently, as did I, for we were tied together, and my fate would be its fate as well. My Lwa was excited to be back among other practitioners. He wanted to celebrate in the old ways with dance, song, and sacrifice. With the approval of my Lwa, I agreed, and the rest of our trip South to San Antonio was spent in silence, for there was nothing left to say.

San Antonio had been a large town last time I had visited.

Now it was a small city. So many people milling about. Horses, roper steam-velocipedes and more modern bi-cycles. Heading towards the center of the old town, the Major made inquiries of a Marshal regarding a telegraph office, and within twenty minutes he was inside sending his telegrams and arranging our passage to Havana, Cuba.

We stayed the night in a proper hotel. We pulled up in our dusty and battered old wagon, which was promptly unloaded of our private crates, and the Major gave a silver coin to the porter to take it to the stable and care for both the horses and the contents. The Major offered his arm, and I took it, while his other arm was occupied by his cane, and we stepped into the most luxurious building I had ever been inside. The floors were covered in thick carpets, the ceilings in coffered and painted panels. There was a restaurant and bar down-stairs, and a porter carried our luggage to our room. The Major excused himself and spoke with a young woman at the desk before escorting me to our room. The porter opened the double doors to a beautiful room painted in soft yellows and pale greens. A large brass bed with a floral quilt commanded the room, proper furniture, all polished and glistening. The porter stepped into an adjoining room, and we could hear water running. I peeked into the room to discover a large copper bath, with pipes delivering water directly into it. I had never seen or even heard of such a thing. I stepped to the tub and dipped my finger into the water, which was hot to the touch. I was spellbound. Finally, the porter poured a measure of scented salts into the water and both my Lwa and

I swooned at the aroma. I would remember this in my next ceremony with my Lwa.

The Major pressed a silver coin into the young man's hand, and he left the room. I looked at the Major for long minutes, taking in his handsome face and recognizing his strength and honor. He smiled and left the room, closing the door behind him. In moments, I had shed the filthy dress and boots I was wearing, and I lowered myself into the warm water. A heavy sigh leaving my body as I immersed.

In minutes, it was clear that the water was going to keep coming, and I had no idea how to stop it. I shouted and slapped the side of the copper tub until the Major rushed in, alarmed at the frantic call. Seeing my peril, he rushed to the tub, shut off the water, then sat on the edge of the tub, laughing in his deep baritone voice. Neither of us felt embarrassed or uncomfortable, at length, I asked for him to undress and join me. We let some of the water out through the hole in the bottom of the tub, he stripped off his breeches and underclothes and he stepped carefully into the tub. Slowly lowering his wrinkled and sagging body into the water, he finally rested opposite and facing me. We closed out eyes and allowed the warm water to soak into us.

I awakened to the Majors strong, long fingers rubbing the soil from my feet. Using a bar he called soap, he lathered each foot and cleansed it before rinsing it in the water, which was becoming browner by the minute.

He raised a wrinkled and white foot to me, and I returned the favor, smiling, and slashing water on him as I cleaned. Carefully, for we were old, and the tub was slippery, we stood and took turns with the soap on each other's body while the tub was emptied, and then refilled. My hair was a matted mess, and I dunked my head underwater, then rubbed the bar soap over it until a brown lather dripped down my forehead and into my eyes, stinging them. I dipped my entire head below the surface, dragging my fingers through my hair before coming up for air, cleaner than I had been since washing in the swamps. The Major did the same and with a final dip, we rinsed each other off and he stepped from the tub, before extending his hand to assist me out. There were with towels that we dried each other off with, and thick cotton robes that we put on. Despite the twice-washing, the towels were still stained brown from the residual grime we did not reach. Last, were slippers made of a lamb's wool that felt like I was floating on air.

We sat on overstuffed chairs, smiles as big as the entire world on our faces, feeling every stress leave our bodies. The spell was broken by a knock on our room door. The major motioned for me to stay seated, and he went to the door, opening it slightly and speaking to the visitor before opening the door to three attendants arriving with parcels and bags. One of the attendants was the young woman the Major had spoken with when we arrived, and she introduced herself as Miss Abernathy. As she talked, she unwrapped the first bag, pulling from it the most beautiful dress of embroidered cotton and lace. She held it up against her body to model it, and I nodded enthusiastically my approval. One by one, she opened dresses for me to preview, while the Major was assisted in gentleman's clothing by the male attendant. Next came the shoes, then the hats, and finally, all the underclothes. I was overwhelmed by the selection and the sheer generosity of this man who never ceased to amaze me. I had no idea how we would travel with all this new wealth until two large steamer trunks were wheeled into the room. The Major and I each selected a proper change of clothing for the following day, and the porters assembled the rest into the various drawers and hangers of the luggage. They turned a key into each of the locks on the trunks and handed the keys over to the Major. He pulled a leather wallet from his folio on the dresser and counted out a stack of bills. With a deep bow, the porters left the room.

I stood smiling what was obviously a ridiculous grin to the major when the door once again knocked, announcing another visitor. Once more the Major opened the door to two valets wheeling a large silver trolley into the room. They walked directly to the table and began unloading the most delicious meal. Meats with sauce poured over, fresh vegetables, pies, cakes, a bottle of red wine, a carafe of strong coffee and a pitcher of water. As quick as they had arrived, they departed with the Majors coin in their pockets.

The major pulled aside my chair and I sat, he joined me on the other side of the table, and we enjoyed a meal unlike any I could have dreamed of.

That night, laying together under white sheets and heavy blankets, I crawled astride him and we made love. It was my first time with a man. I was one hundred and two years to his seventy, and it felt like we were youngsters on a date. Such a perfect night, and such a memorable time. I was resolved to enjoy every second, because I knew it would not last.

†††

We departed for Galveston two days later. At the hotel desk, a porter whom we had been most generous to whispered something to Major Dunston that caused the blood to drain from his face. He pressed another coin into the porter's hand and uttered a thanks, then brusquely took my elbow and ushered me to a waiting carriage. Our luggage had been sent ahead to the Sunset Limited train which provided service from San Antonio to Galveston Harbor. As our carriage sped away from the hotel, I could see two Marshals arriving on horseback, dismounting with guns drawn.

We sped along Hoefgen Avenue to the train station. Our carriage driver, alerted to our urgency, pulled the carriage down a side street to a platform frequented by those of celebrity or wealth with private train carriages. He stepped down from his seat and quickly folded down the stairs of the carriage before opening the door to allow the Major and I to exit, no easy feat in our aged condition. He led us to our car, and the butler then assisted us up the steep stairs to inside. Once there, there was nothing to do but for the butler to pour the Major a crystal glass of whiskey, and for me a small, fluted crystal of port. We sat nervously while the train boarded. With a whistle, we could hear the conductor crying "all-aboard", and we could hear the clatter of linkages as the engine struggled to pull forward against the weight of 14 carriages. Slowly we inched out of the station, gathering steam as we went. I could see the Major relax, but I could not, for my Lwa was seething and restless. This was always a bad sign. I knew that we were still being pursued.

Minutes before they came into our car, I alerted the Major, and he alerted the butler. "Do not, under any circumstance allow anyone into this carriage," were his instructions. The man, fiercely loyal to the passengers of his car, whomever they should be at the time, nodded and placed a bar across the door, prohibiting entry. We soon heard the telltale rattle of someone on the other side attempting to gain entry and failing. We could hear the muffled cry to open, but the butler had fetched a shotgun and stood sentry at the door. It was unlikely that anyone could breach the door with the bar across it, but he was standing ready, for the sake of his passenger and the certain additional payment he would receive for his vigilance.

While the door rattled and banged, a Marshall had climbed atop the carriage roof and come back down on the other end. He casually opened the door behind us, gun drawn, and announced our arrest.

With four Marshalls now in our carriage as it sped across the Texas landscape, it was clear that these young, strong men needed no guns to manage these two ancient and feeble old characters. They helped themselves to our liquor and food, and a wiry, rangy looking Marshal stepped up to the Major, pointing a slab of beef at him, "you live good for a criminal" he said. The major sat quietly, unperturbed. "Your lady friend here is under arrest. We're sending her on to Baton Rouge to stand trial for murder. What's your role in this game Sir?"

The Major looked straight in the young man's eye with

a steely confidence that betrayed his age. This woman is my wife. She has never been to Baton Rouge, nor has she committed any crime. You, sir, are mistaken and neither of us will be joining you on your visit to the State of Louisiana.

The Marshal then looked at me. "Is that right? Well perhaps I want to hear that from this woman herself."

The Major spoke for me, "As I said, you have the wrong woman."

The Marshall sat on his heels, coming eye to eye with me. "Nope" he said, "we caught us the witch of the swamp. She's gonna stand trail and they will hang her".

I glanced to see the Marshal, as cool as winter sitting there, knowing something I did not. I could feel my Lwa, coiled inside me like a viper ready to strike.

"Those stories are over a hundred years old. Does she look that old to you"? asked the Major.

"She's old awright", slurred the Marshal. "Aint for me to say nohow. The judge give us this writ to bring her in, and bring her we shall".

†††

Hours later, the train pulled into the station at Galveston. The Major placed several bills into the hand of the Butler. A black man who seemed white as a sheet. His neatly starched white tuxedo blouse spattered with red mist. His hands shaking mightily. The Major and I stepped out of our salon car and directly into a waiting hansome carriage, pulled by a beautiful black mare. As prearranged, our luggage would be carted to the steamer ship *Cassandra* and placed aboard in our room.

We would see no other Marshals. The Butler was a quick-thinking man who had disposed of the scraps of flesh, bone, and hair from the carriage, and mopped and cleaned it down completely, before boarding the first train bound for Chicago.

As for the Major, he seemed entirely unmoved by the arrival of my Lwa, or the furious attack that followed. I had whispered to him that something horrible was going to happen, and that I needed him to neither interrupt, nor panic. He was to sit still in his chair and not react. He looked at me questioningly but said nothing. His fingers gripped the arms of the chair, and he held tight ready for anything. In this moment, I felt closer than ever to the Major. Such trust and faith he had in me! Without question, he accepted my warning and trusted the outcome. Once done, he sat trembling in his chair, his eyes wide with alarm, but no fright or panic was evident, just surprise. I rested my hand on his and told him that all would be explained on the boat, and that too was final.

Our travel would be far less comfortable, for as our ship left harbor, the winds began to rise, blowing to the Northeast. This was in our favor as we left Galveston Harbor and slipped between Galveston and Pelican Island. The peninsula at For San Jacinto blocked much of the wind as we approached the Gulf of Mexico. But once we sailed into the open gulf, we were hit broadside by a gale of wind. The Captain was unperturbed. He had navigated these waters in winds worse than this for decades, and he simply turned the boat into the wind and put her on a heading South-West. We would lose speed towards our goal but would stay on course towards Havana.

I, of course, spent a lifetime in the sheltered waters and

open lakes of the Louisiana Bayou. If blown off course, it was only a matter of making land and waiting the storms out, but here in open water, endless as far as the eye could see, I was fiercely afraid for my safety and the Majors.

He stood still as stone, being my consummate protector. He would not allow himself to show fear lest it stir fear in me, and so I was comforted, if only by the stoic and brave nature of this fine man.

For hours we steamed ahead, yet we could still see land off our stern and starboard sides. The Major went to the pilot-house to inquire with the captain, who noted that we were indeed losing ground to the wind. We were blowing Eastward and we little more than twenty miles off Port Arthur. Still, we were offshore far enough that we could continue to steam ahead and when the wind subsided, we would resume course.

Night fell and the wind increased. It was not in gusts, but a steady pressure against our hull and side. The moonless night of the gulf was pitch black. We had no landmark or bearing to understand where we were, so we trusted our captain and crew, and stayed in our small cabin on the starboard side of the boat. The side taking the direct wind. The sound was terrible! It was as if giants were pounding their fists on the steel hull. It was relentless, and as hour after hour passed, neither the Major, nor I was able to sleep. Hours before dawn, I felt my Lwa stir. It was as if he were sniffing the air for something familiar. It showed neither fear nor expectation, just restless energy.

Dawn broke with a wind that had been unresolved through the night. We had been blown steadily to the East, despite our best efforts. The Major and I carefully made our way to the rail on the leeward side of the boat. The side sheltered from the wind by the superstructure of the ship. Even here, the wind whipped our hair and clothing like a flag in a storm. It was here that I saw the Atchafalaya off our starboard side. Inland, far from the delta of the Atchafalaya River would be the towns of Calumet and Morgan City. We were being blown right into the Atchafalaya bay and we would eventually run aground one of the hundreds of small islands protruding from the bayou one the border of Texas and Louisiana. Unless this wind stopped soon, we would be shipwrecked back in the same place I had escaped from so many years ago. Deep inside me I could feel my excitement of my Lwa. To this day, I do not believe that my Lwa caused this catastrophe, but I also know that it was glad to be home.

We did run aground some miles North of the entrance to Fourleague Bay. The same inlet I had exited to escape the endless swamp of the bayou. I could spot Turn Point to the North and Fox point to the South. We were on the peninsula, on the coast just beyond Alligator Cut. With the open water of the Atchafalaya bay to the West, we could see open water clear to the horizon. We were in the middle of nowhere, forty miles from Morgan city by water, that being the closest assistance.

It was decided that the Captain would take two of the lifeboats and five men for each to row. They would set off North, to South Point, at the inlet to Fourleague bay, then attempt the treacherous crossing to Halters Island. If they made it, they could traverse north-west to the entrance of the Atchafalaya river, where they may be able to flag down a passing ship. If not, they would need to row upstream against the current for twenty miles to Morgan City. It could take a week or more for them to get there, and two to three more for them to come back with another ship to rescue us. Seven to ten days.

The Major quickly took control of the day-to-day work of

the ship. Food was rationed, tasks were assigned, both on and off the boat, and sentries were posted to prevent pirates or wild creatures to board us.

I watched as the Major assumed his leadership role with confidence. I asked to go ashore with a small crew of men and women to reconnoiter, and after assuring the Major that I was comfortable in this environment, he allowed me to lead my small party ashore.

For the first time in many years, my feet touched the soft, moist earth of the bayou. It felt odd to wear shoes, and to the surprise of my group, I shucked them off and let my toes sink into the boggy grasses. Closing my eyes, I felt the earth come up to greet me as my Lwa and I swayed in the breeze like the tall cane around us. When I opened my eyes, it was to the gathered group of passengers who were enthralled by my absolute joy and pleasure of the moment. It is so rare for any of us to experience this in our lifetimes, and to even observe it was as close as many would come. My happiness was amplified by my Lwa, who bade me to dance and sing for him, but I could not, for that would be too conspicuous. A reserved joy was appropriate, and my beaming smile showed all what they needed to know.

A few of the others took off their shoes as well, digging toes into the wet earth, but unaccustomed to barefoot travel, they quickly regretted it and sought to clean the mud and debris from their feet to put their shoes back on. I alone walked with bare feet across grass and stone, completely immune to the uneven land around me. I gazed up to the ships rail and saw the Major smiling down at me. He could see what others had seen, and it filled him with happiness to know my complete immersion in this wilderness.

I rounded up my small crew and hiked across the shore and up into the trees. One moment we were seen by all on the ship, the next, the bayou had swallowed us up.

My companions were nervously excited, but my confidence buoyed them, and they accepted the adventure for what it was. I pointed out salamanders, and snakes and spiders and other such life that was completely invisible to the uninitiated. We saw a large alligator who had come inland in search of food and was feasting on a small deer. The assembled stared wide-eyed, but we moved along, leaving the alligator to its meal. I began collecting herbs and plants along the way, filling up the baskets and bags each person carried. With a carefully thrown rocks, I had killed three rabbits, and I had even throttled an iguana, which would make a wonderful soup. All the while, my guests were completely enamored with my woodcraft skill. To me, this was simply gathering an evening meal.

Making a large sweeping loop of about one mile, we returned to the ship with our baskets and bags overflowing. Once clean shoes were now muddy and scratched. Trousers splattered with mud and skirts tinted brown at the bottoms. Sweat ran from our brows and a smile was on every face. We had shipwrecked and missed our assigned destination, but we had enjoyed a great adventure together.

That night, as the passengers sampled my rabbit and iguana stew and nearly cleaned out the ships liquor inventory, we took turns telling tales of our lives, sharing fears, adventures, wishes, and joys. At midnight, I gave into my Lwa's pleadings and stood amidst our guests. I raised my hands high and began dancing slowly, showing my love for this moment. I spun, dipped, and twirled. All was quiet and enraptured as I danced for my Lwa. At present, the Major stood and came to me, bowing low and taking my hand. We waltzed together in the lantern light, spinning and holding each other like lovers. Two by two, the others came to join us and soon, the deck was filled with people singing, dancing, and making merry. I could feel my Lwa and the Major both bursting with happiness, and I was content.

†††

Marooned on this spit of land, the first two days were filled with activity and cooperation. As time went on, tempers flared, opinions became more pronounced and a fight over control of leadership began to form. It was not from the men, who could clearly see the leadership quality in the Major and appreciated his role, but among the women. Petty, impatient and emotional, nothing was ever good enough, right enough, or done to their satisfaction. In the night it was too cold, in the day to hot. The rationing of water had curbed their toilette and cleaning regimens. They made demands of their husbands who could do no less than seek to quell their unhappiness by bickering with the Major.

The solution was quite simple, the Major and I stepped off the boat and into the bayou on the third morning and left the passengers to fend for themselves.

It was the first opportunity the Major had to explore our peninsula, and he followed me at his best pace, which was slow at best. He had trouble raising his right leg, and his cane was forever catching on vines or sinking into the mud, but he did not complain, quite the opposite, the walk in nature was doing marvels for his countenance. There was a spring in his wobbly step, and he whistled a tune of the Union while we walked. The noise startled me, for in my hundred plus years, I had heard a whistle only a few times. I stopped and watched the form of his mouth and the tempo of his breath. It is nearly impossible to smile and whistle at the same time, yet the Major did his best, and soon I was attempting to mimic his sounds. Pushing air though pursed lips as he gently tutored me. Within a few moments I had made a squeaky whistling sound and I erupted into a cackle of laughter. As we walked on, I tried for over twenty minutes before I made my first real whistle. Tears came to my eyes, and I fought the smiles that interrupted my whistling noises. As morning passed to late afternoon, I whistled nonstop, learning to make tone and sound changes, trying to replicate music I had heard, or making my own music. I came to a waterway blocking our path and turned to the Major. But the Major was gone. How long had I walked without looking back? How many hours or miles had I been absorbed in my own pleasure, without care or concern for my companion. I called out, but there was no response. I turned on my heel and ran back through the grass to find my man.

I was an adept tracker, and the bent grass and footprints in the mud were as easy as following a road to me. I ran on, for well over a mile, the panic in me growing. Twice I had seen the telltale belly slide of alligator crossing the path I had already traveled. The sounds of the bayou were amplified with my terror. I came to the last place the Majors footprints met mine. A place I could clearly see he had stood and looked around, trampling the grasses in all directions looking for my trail. He had chosen poorly and had walked off in a direction that led South.

I followed at a brisk pace, now conserving my energy, and listing for his whistle or words. A quarter mile, half mile... and then I found him. He was sitting on a fallen cypress, right leg crossed over the left in casual comfort. He turned at the sound of me running up the trail and he smiled.

My chest heaving, my blood pounding, I could have killed him for that smile, but instead I rushed to him and wrapped my arms around him, holding him tight as to never let him go. He returned the embrace and then looked me in the eyes. I could see the concern and fear in his eyes then. I knew he had grave concern for both him and me, but he would not let it show lest it worry me more. Lest it show a lack of confidence in me, and I loved him more for it.

It is never safe to travel the bayou after dark. There are panthers, and alligators and all manner of nocturnal hunters. The sun had gone down and night was full upon us. On the horizon, we could see a halo of light and we followed it, stepping over stone and bush in a stumbling, blind lurch. We discovered every ship lantern had been moved to the shoreside rail. A bonfire assembled on the beach and every passenger looking into the dark in search of us.

As we came out of the darkness and into the light, a cheer erupted and a stream of passengers came down the gangplank, surrounding us and providing assistance. They led us to the galley and fed us a warm broth, then sent us to our cabin to wash up. Their fear for their friends had eclipsed all complaint amongst each other. They came together as a unified group to wish their friend's home. We felt their love and happiness at our return. We could feel their relief that the solid, unifying presence that the Major and I embodied had returned. They needed our confidence to boost their own.

Two days later, the captain and his men returned in an old tramp steamer. We could see the column of smoke from her stacks long before we could spot the boat itself. The captain had his original two boats lowered from the side of the steamer, and he returned to our boat, although now there were twelve men in the boats instead of the original ten.

They pulled up to the beach and disembarked. The captain shouted orders to the crew to ready the boats to be loaded back on the Cassandra, while the two new men, both large and ominous, walked directly to the gangplank and came aboard.

A few passengers bade them welcome, but they were all business and did not engage in idle conversation. They were hunting the Major and I. My Lwa felt it before we did, but I held it in check, waiting to see how this would play out. No words were spoken. They simply took us by the shoulders and turned us around, securing the handcuffs to our wrists. The passengers were dumbfounded. This quickly turned to anger as their elderly friends were being treated as criminals. The crowd began to form around the constables, and they turned us to the assembled. The man who held the Major spoke clear and loudly. "These people are wanted for murder in Texas.

The woman is also wanted for murder in Louisiana. We don't want no trouble, so don't give us none".

With that, we were led, gently but firmly, down the gangplank, and to a waiting skiff that would return us to the tramp steamer. The passengers did not resist, nor did they come to our aid. They watched as we were rowed across out and hoisted unceremoniously into the steamer.

We were ushered down a corridor and into a stateroom where we were locked in tight, with the two constables remaining outside the door.

From the small port hole, we watched as a large rope was rowed to the stranded Cassandra, and the steamer threw her screws into reverse, pulling the Cassandra off the shore just as easy as you please.

The captain of the Cassandra wasted no time bringing up her steam and continuing his course to Havana. We could not see the Cassandra from our vantage, but we could hear her chuffing off into the distance. I could almost see the dark muddy bottom of this shallow shoreline churning up dark rich mud from the bottom. I breathed in deep, hoping to capture the smell of my beloved swamp, but smelled only the oil, coal and sweat of a hundred bodies that had lain on these bunks in this wreck of a room.

The Major was thoughtful. He was a careful strategist and had been in difficult situations before. Me, I was just getting angry. I was fueled with the ferocity of my Lwa. The Major rested his hand on mine, as if to lend me his strength, and it helped. We would be in Morgan City by morning, we needed to think.

When I woke, it was to the cold, dead body of the Major next to me. His body spooning mine on the narrow bunk, his arm draped protectively over me. He had passed quietly, so kind and gentle so as not to disturb the sleep he felt I needed. Such was the generosity of this man.

But now I had no hand to cover mine. I had no one to still my spirit and calm my soul. I dressed in trousers and a loose-fitting shirt. A shirt fit for the humidity and damp of the swamp. I left my shoes under the edge of the bed, for I would no longer need them. I closed my eyes and spoke to my Lwa. Level and articulate, I described exactly what I wanted and expected. I could feel every muscle and tendon in my body tighten. I could feel the blood pumping through every vein. My breath was deep and steady as I unleashed my Lwa. It came with furor and frenzy, blasting the steel door from hits hinges, and obliterating the men standing watch over our room. Each one raining down in a light mist of red as I walked toward the pilothouse.

I entered to the captain smoking a pipe and his pilot steering the large wheel. The pipe dropped from his mouth as he stared wide-eyed at the old woman before him, bathed in a mist of blood and alive with a crackling energy that made the hairs on my head stand on end like a medusa.

I looked to the pilot, and he evaporated into red mist, coating the wheel and windshield of the pilothouse. I turned back to the Captain and smiled, pointing to his charts. We would chart a new course for Fourleague Bay. I was going home.

†††

The captain had wiped the windshield with his sleeve to

clear the glass but achieved only smearing the blood around. Watching me every moment, he stepped to a cabinet and removed a large cotton rag, and poured his coffee over it, then cleaned the windshield as best he could.

Certainly, he had a pistol somewhere in here, but what he had witnessed was not anything that he could kill with a gun. He did not understand what I was, but he understood what I was capable of. He complied with shaking hands and nervous glances.

He steered us back toward the inlet at Fourleague. We would travel some thirty miles during the day, and we entered the Blue Hammock Bayou channel to lost lake by early evening. Nearly impossible to navigate during the day, and insane to travel at night, I demanded he do his best, and he began to cruise up the narrow channel. By evening, we had arrived at the Narrows where the Violin Bayou splits to the South and Marchant Lake lies to the East. In failing light, he traveled slow, watching for fallen cypress, sand bars and other hazards. Soon, the shadows had obscured virtually all visibility. He was piloting on sheer instinct and experience. We hugged the shore into Lake Washa under a half-moon, and into the open water of Lake Merchant under starlight. Once in open water, he sank into his Captains chair and wept. I felt no remorse or sympathy. I was beyond these feelings. I had been robbed of everything I ever loved by people who desired to own, control, or punish me. I would take it no more.

Morning brought us to Bayou Chevreau. So close to home I could smell it. I had the Captain run up into the northernmost channel until the channel was so narrow and shallow, we ran aground. We were deep in the belly of the swamps. In places this old captain never even knew existed.

Together we lowered a rope ladder over the side, and the Captain lowered himself a few steps before assisting me down from below. Step by step, this fifty-something year old man and a woman of well over a century. As his feet touched the ground, I could feel in him the desire to run, but he did not. No matter how dire, he was a man of integrity who would not abandon a woman to these wilds.

My own bare feet touched damp soil and I could feel the energy rising through the ground and into my body. This was my home. How foolish I was to ever be chased from it. How foolish were those who would have ever chased me. Never again. I was home and home I would stay.

Released by me, the Captain scrambled back up the rope ladder, quickly hauling it aboard, lest I desire to come back to the ship. He hurriedly brought her up to steam and threw her into reverse.

By this time, I was several hundred yards away. Deep in the swamp where I could not see the ship but could hear her engines straining. I let my Lwa free, like a man turns loose his guard dog, and soon heard the explosion of the boilers and felt the hot wind of impact at my back. I did not turn to see the havoc I had wrought, I only walked on, searching the shore for a pirogue or cabin. Both of which I found abandoned some two hours later.

I spent two nights in the shanty domicile. Holes in the roof and rain dripping all around me. I was too elated to care. I danced and sang to my Lwa through the night, only stopping of sheer exhaustion. I lay in the darkness on a wood-slat floor, smiling to myself, and remembering the warm embrace of the Major.

†††

As I came upon the dock I had built so many years before I took note of the fine quality of the three pirogues tied to her. I could see the well-worn track leading up through the cypress toward the meadow. Others had taken up residence in my home. Would I ask them to politely leave, or would I simply take it by force? I had no plan, only the fierce drive to reclaim what was mine.

I tied off to the dock and stepped onto well-worn planks. She had been well cared for in my absence. Whomever had move in, took pride in their home.

Where once was a slippery mud path, was now carefully constructed steps, each designed to shed the water. The path was carefully trimmed, looking more of a manicured trail than the trampled earth of my day.

At the edge of the meadow, I looked up the hill to see my domicile. It was freshly painted and immaculate. It was a beautiful home amidst the most comforting of settings. I stood for long minutes, thinking about Temmy Rowan, of the many who had come for help and the many who had come to harm. An entire lifetime of experiences came flooding back. My eyes welled with tears of happiness. I could feel the courage of my life here. Of the strength it took to carves this home out of the marsh and bayou.

I stood in appreciation for those who had taken it upon themselves to be the caretakers of my home. To care for it as if it were their own. They would be richly rewarded for their good work.

As I walked up the meadow, a woman stepped from the house and onto the porch. She had on a cotton shift, and was barefoot, like me. She called out, and a man came to stand by her side. Lithe, strong, and relaxed, he stood with his arm draped over her shoulder in solidarity.

Coming closer, I offered out my greeting, which earned a startled and frightened rigidity in both persons. Her eyes were wide with fright, but also held bitterness and anger. His face turned to stone but held a resolve of a man who was raised in these swamps and had fought and scraped to hold onto any-thing he could call his own. He was like every inhabitant of the bayou, determined to survive and thrive.

As I stepped up to the steps leading to the porch, she said, "I always knew you would come back". Her voice trembled with tension. "Whatch you want?", said the man. He had grown up with stories of the Swamp Witch and had recon-ciled them all down to being just stories. He would not be afraid until I gave him reason to be.

I stood there, looking every bit the part of a lost soul in the bayou. My feet bleeding from being in shoes too many years, mud and debris caked my feet, ankles, and shins. My shift was tattered from acacia thorns grabbing at the edges. My hair hung low down my back and carried all manner of debris and seeds from the walk through heavy brush. He looked down on me like a property owner trying to determine if he has been trespassed, or if it is just a visitor come to call.

I gave my best smile and said that I appreciated them

taking care of my home for me while I was gone. The woman harumphed and the man stood up straight and tall. Looking down from the porch, he motioned with his hands for me to shoo-away. He said "this is our home now. You ain't got no claim to it".

I smiled my biggest smile, showing teeth that were brown from age and use. Long teeth that had black down in the roots. It was meant to be comforting, but it only aggravated the situation. I pointed to each of them and gave an animated, shoo-shoo movement of my hands to them, shooing them off down the meadow trail.

The man then stepped off the porch, intent on shoving me away from the house. I stood still as a stone. As the palm of his hand met with my chest, and as his forward momentum carried the weight of his body into me, my Lwa dissolved him as he fell through me. A light ash fell from my old cotton dress as the breeze fluttered it in the wind. Expecting resistance, he had stepped off the porch and just kept coming, until just shins, ankles and feet were laying on the ground in front of me.

The look on my own face was one of total pleasure. Of rapture, for I would never have known or believed that my Lwa was capable of such a feat. Yes, he had given me strength to kill a man, even tear one limb from limb. The moment I had destroyed the men aboard the tramp steamer had been one of explosive force. It seemed to me that this was all a dance of violence. In the moment, I realized that it did not need to be violent at all. It could be as graceful and calming as a gentle breeze, and that is just how it felt as I swept the woman from the porch with only a glance and watched her body float like a feather as it dissolved away into dust. It was rapturous, and I encouraged the breeze to carry their remains far out into the bayou. Cleaning house.

I took the porch steps one by one and stepped into my home. Clean, arranged, uncluttered. Fresh bread on the stove, and a stew cooking in the iron pot. It could not have been a better homecoming feast.

THE WITCH WARS

I would find out much later what preceded the next several decades. Following our flight from Texas, news had spread like wildfire about the capture and escape of the Swamp Witch. It was Andra Simmon's herself who arrived by train with the full weight and finance of the New York Herald behind her, investigating the story, interviewing witnesses, and crafting her tale to spellbind the masses.

She followed the story to the pier, then aboard the Cassandra. After the Cassandra, the story had reached a dead end. The tramp steamer and her crew were never found or heard from again, leaving the tale hanging in the air like an axe about to fall.

Like the good reporter she was, Andra would return to the scene of the crime, finding herself down in Dulac, Cocodrie, and even as close as Dularge, just a few miles from me. But she could find no evidence of me. She found no witness, story, or any person willing to guide her into the swamp to where I had previously lived. She threw down her coin, but the swamp world was divided into two camps. Those who feared me, and those who missed me, for as evil as my legend was, many remembered me as the only medical help for miles around.

They recalled me healing their parents, or grandparents. They had purchased a potion, or asked for a miracle, or favor. To some I was a monster better left under the bed, to others, I was a savior returned to help those in desperate need.

And they came to me. Slow and cautious at first. A pair of eyes watching from the bottom of the meadow to see if I would show myself. A tentative step up the meadow trail, only to turn and run, but eventually, the truly helpless and ill would bravely march up the hill, lay down their coin and seek my healing.

As news spread that I had returned, and I was there to heal, more people came. They came with coin or barter. They came with humility and no small amount of hubris. They came head bowed and asking, never demanding. In return, My Lwa and I worked in the open. No longer did we hide in our ounfò to prepare. My ounfò was my home and my surgery was once again my kitchen table. When they were ready, I would begin to dance and sign. I wore my headdress of freshly gathered feathers. I would slit a baby alligator from chin to tail and bleed it over a shallow tin platter. Through all of this, my patients were terrified, but resolute. They had heard the tales and knew what to expect. They no longer thought of me as a healer, but as the witch. A witch that could erase their pain, or help them walk, or cure their cancers and ulcers. A witch who would close their wounds and clean infections. I was a miracle worker, and I was unmolested for years.

Of course, the nature of man is rooted in greed. While the people of the swamp would respect me, the loose tongues in the saloons and whore houses would talk. The unscrupulous, desperate, and hungry would travel far and wide, retelling the tale to gain some form of notoriety. The war began with rural preachers who had come to my home in the name of a God they never believed in but profited from. So comfortable had we become in our life that the first came right up to my door before my Lwa was alerted. He carried a large bronze cross, while three adherents, farmers all, carried shotguns and pistols. My Lwa dispatched each of them, and I threw their weapons into the swamp.

Within weeks a second group came, then a third, emboldened by the seeming lack of threat or danger. Men had gone in and had not come out. This left their fate unknown, which was not threatening at all. Thus, I reasoned with my Lwa that we must change our strategy.

Within a few more weeks, three pirogues, tied together stern to bow, floated into Dularge. Inside were ten men and two women. They were stripped naked, and the outer flesh had been burned from the muscle and bone, leaving a charred, red body behind. Each was seated in the boat as if they had just been poled into shore. One woman in the last boat was sitting stock still and straight backed. She was naked as the others, but her skin and hair was as white as a cloud, and her hands were balled up tight into fists. She repeated the same line over and over, unable to stop herself.

"stop, stop, stop, stop".....

All was quiet for weeks following. Even the ill stayed away, preferring to suffer in their homes rather than to brave the anger of the Swamp Witch.

But eventually they did come. A regiment of regular Army,

from the Garrison in New Orleans. Young, fresh-faced teen boys, old, grizzled, and whiskered career men, and a polished, unseasoned officer fresh from West Point Military Academy in New York. He would make his mark by starting his career with eliminating the threat that had plagued the *witch bayou*, as my Swamp home had become known.

The Army had determined that this should be a publicity campaign and the soldiers were followed closely by a trail of reporters and interested parties. The lessons learned by the Commanders of the Confederacy had long faded memory, the officers lay in their graves, taking their advice and nightmares with them.

It was Tedrê who came to me alone, a boy of 13. I had cured both his mother and father of typhus. I had bled and stitched up his leg when it has festered to the size of his head. I was known to him, and he came speaking for an entire community who feared for my safety. "They are coming", said he. "They are coming in two days' time to capture you and take you to trial". I thanked Tedrê and gave him a shiny dollar for himself, and a snapping turtle étouffée to share with his parents. I sent him on his way and began my preparations.

I spent the rest of the day gathering driftwood and dried vines from across the bayou. I was an old woman, yet I could lift and drag as well as any strong young man. I built a large pile in the middle of the meadow. That night, under a three-quarter moon, I lit the pyre and fanned it to life. The wood was moist in the bayou humidity, but it slowly caught. It would never be a roaring blaze, but it's coals and embers would last till dawn.

I began with a slow, intense dance for my Lwa. It was not like those of the past, where I flailed and writhed in a frenzy. This was rhythmic and deep. I pounded my feet into the earth, one at a time. My body jerked, as if shot by a musket. My eyes shut tight in concentration.

My Lwa was as dark and ominous as I was. He was a stalking panther, a slithering snake. He was all the things of the swamp that we fear. And in his predator state, he called forth all the most feared things of the swamp. They flew into the air, slithered into the water, and bound through the cypress and moss to our small spit of land. As they arrived, they too swayed and danced with my Lwa and I. And then I did the unexpected. With the sparks flying from my bonfire, high into the air, and my Lwa stalking, and the predators of the swamp circling, I called to the Spirit of Maka. The fire roared to life and my Lwa shrieked a terrible shriek. From the flames stepped a ghostly apparition of Maka, naked and shimmering like wind through the tall bayou grasses. With him was his Lwa, smoky and foul. He came to me and wrapped his arms around me, and I him. We held each other for long minutes, remembering our connection and our companionship. Remembering the bullet that pierced his head, and the blood that ran down his face and belly.

I took Maka's hand and raised it high. Our Lwa raised their club-like fists high into the air with us. Once again, the flamed rose like a torch fanned by the winds of a hurricane, creating a tornado of fire. From the fire came my mother and father, together with their Lwa. Where the Lwa of Maka and I were black and ominous, filled with fierce anger and frenzied fury, the Lwa of my parents were cool and white, like steam. They were rational and cunning. They were looking about, measuring our resources, and creating a strategy. There was a place for all of this in this fight.

Wrapping my arms around my parents, I wept. They were tears of joy and tears of sorrow. As we held each other, I could feel their positive energy, their good spirit. They were here for justice, Maka for revenge, and I for the right to live in peace.

†††

Morning found me alone in the meadow. Wet mud caked to the side of my face where it lay in the soft meadow grasses. My limbs stiff from laying on the hard earth, but I could feel a strength and energy that was far beyond anything I had known in my lifetime. I could feel the presence of my parents, of Maka and of the Lwa, all residing within me. I could feel the combined magic of all of us, barely contained within my soul. With a tentative test I raised an old, crooked finger to the edge of my meadow and an ancient cypress burst into a million splinters. I had barely tried, and it had cost me none of my energy or reserves. Raising both arms, I drug fallen cypress and boulders across the meadow and thrust it like cannon fire to the far edge of my meadow land. I had strength of one hundred men, and the magic to move mountains.

Turning on bare feet, I walked down to the dock, stripped off my tattered cotton shift, and dove headfirst into the swamp. I washed my body and my soul that morning, wading out of the tea-stained water as clean the day I was born. I stood on the dock for long minutes, allowing the morning warmth to seep into my bones. My face, arms and feet were baked brown by the sun, but my cotton frock had left the rest of me pasty white and nearly translucent. Blue veins stood out on my breasts and legs. I rather liked the look, and with a thought, the entirety of my body took on a ghostly translucent pallor. I wanted them to see the Swamp Witch when they arrived. I wanted them to see me for who and what I was, an immortal, possessed by the spirits of my kin and my Lwa. I wanted them to know what was coming. I wished into existence a long cape of raven's feathers. Black as sin and soft and light as gossamer. The effect of the black cape against my white skin was startling, and I felt it showed two sides of me. Within the black was certain death. It was pain and suffering, brimstone, and darkness. Within the white was hope and forgiveness. It was opportunity that you would want to grab, but probably would not. Either way, I would have my day.

My Lwa let me know of their arrival long before they made land at my small dock. I sat in my rocking chair on my porch, smoking a small clay pipe, feeling the breeze move through the humidity.

I knew when they came ashore. The normal cacophony of the birds, frogs and insects of the bayou went quiet and still as they approached my docks. A few moments later, the screams of terror assaulted the quiet. The alligator groaned as they fed, and high-pitched roar of the panthers as they dropped from the trees onto the men below. I could rear the report of musket fire as the men fought for survival. If I listened closely, I could even hear the hiss of the cottonmouth and copperhead and the rattle of the Eastern diamondback and the timber rattler. Eagles and Osprey dropped from the sky with their terrible screech as their talons sought eye and throat. Such a glorious cacophony of sound in a previously quiet morning.

The fighting receded, the men having returned to their boats, and poled out into deeper water. I could hear the wailings of the injured on the shore, crying out for their brothers to return and save them. But their cries were contrasted by the fresh lieutenant shouting for retreat. The cries from the boats receded into the distance, and one by one, the cries from shore went silent as the bodies were drug into the bayou. A feast for the victors.

I could not tell you how many men came to the docks that day, nor can I tell you how many died. Tedré had fetched me some canned peaches and a copy of the New York Herald that had made its way to Dulac. The cover story was of the assault on the lair of the Swamp Witch and the terrible vengeance she took on the soldiers. It was written by Andra Simmon's. I could feel my Lwa's regret at not killing her in Texas. The spectacle was now magnified a thousand times, for the embarrassment of the Government of the United States required a demonstration of submission. A new headline must be written to show the power and might of the country's military machine.

It took a full month for the soldiers to return. The lieutenant had been replaced by a man of hardened battle and fresh reinforcements. Fighting men who had seen the countless campaigns against the Mexicans, the Indians, and some even foreign wars. These were not fresh recruits; they were honest to god soldiers.

Tedré came to me again to let me know they had

bivouacked at Dularge. The men of New Orleans were dressed for the mission, but those from Northern States were wearing heavy wool and cotton uniforms and were terribly hot and uncomfortable. They slept poorly in the heat, humidity, and mosquitos. Many drank the bad water and had fallen ill with dysentery or had become feverish. There were over two hundred soldiers at the camp, but Tedré figured that less than one hundred would be in fighting shape.

I thanked Tedré again and paid him well for the groceries and information.

I surveyed my meadow home. It was a place of peace, already interrupted by violence. It was my home, not a battlefield. I was in no mood to wait for these men to come to me, only to stain my beautiful home, I would take the fight to them.

†††

I walked to my dock early in the morning poling my pirogue towards Dularge. Outside of town, I poled to shore and willed a large alligator to come to me. It was there that I slit his belly and poured warm, wet blood over the bow of my pirogue. Wearing only my raven cape over my naked, skeletal body, and with red blood coating my arms to the elbows, I poled into Dularge in the hottest part of the day, on the hottest day of the year.

It took only moments for the people of Dularge to congregate at the shoreline. They had come to witness the Swamp Witch come to battle the mighty army. Some of the gathered crossed themselves to ward off evil, but most of these people had cause to be healed by me at one time of another during their lives, and these people bowed low as I passed.

I stood stoically in the boat, perfectly balanced and perfectly poised. Someone must have run ahead to the soldier's camp, as I began to see the men run to the shore, lining up to see the old woman who came to them.

By the time I reached the dock, lined with row after row of pirogues, the entire camp had assembled at the shore. They were in various stages of undress, few if any had weapons. They saw no threat. They were afraid of the wild predators of the swamps, but in me they saw only a feeble old lady.

I stood mid-stream, waiting for men to move boats aside so that I could land mine. As I came to the dock, a sturdy man of some forty odd years took hold of my bow and tied off my bow line. As I stepped off my boat, he extended his hand to assist me, as a gentleman would. I would remember this kindness before the day was over.

With the men crowding around me, I walked up to the shore to present myself to the commander. He was mid-fifties, grey at the temples, well-muscled and tired. He had been fighting rough and violent all his adult life. He had earned the respect and command of his men, and now he was reduced to leading two hundred men against an old lady. He was humiliated and his dysentery was not helping his mood.

I stood before him, and he looked me up and down. I must have looked theatrical to him rather than menacing, for he smiled in a tolerant manner, and waited for me to say something, anything.

This was the moment that would define the next evolution

of battle. I could ease into it and elevate the fear until it was an all-out bloodbath, or I could simply show this man what he was up against and let him choose for himself.

With a contingent of reporters and photographers off to the side, poised with pen and camera, and a seasoned military man, backed by two hundred of America's finest, I released the visage of Maka to my left. A ghost of a black man, fierce and menacing. To my right, the visages of my parents, calm and focused. Behind each of us, our Lwa, as tall as trees, and far more fearsome than any of the predators of the swamps. The men scattered and ran. The Commander stood slack jawed and frozen in place. The photographers, always the professionals, shot picture after picture, while the reporters wrote furiously in their notebooks, memorializing the moment.

I began to dance with my hands, sweeping my arms in great arcs. I spoke with a commanding voice, communicating as clear and succinct. I claimed the title of the Swamp Witch, the Sorciére. I introduced myself as a woman who sought only to heal but had been hunted. I introduced my companions as those hunted and killed by men like those present. I communicated that in this moment, I could walk away, return to my home, and live in peace, or I could annihilate this army and any other that followed. The choice was the Commanders to make.

But it was made for him. A lone soldier scared witless had fetched his musket and shot a round at me from behind.

My Lwa easily parried the shot and bore down on the man like a freight train, cleaving him cleanly in two. The moment was lost to the frenzy of the Lwa. Too long deprived of their more violent tendencies, they launched at the men, burning, slicing, pummeling, and destroying with abandon.

I was beyond angry. I was in a furious trance, and I allowed the Lwa their moment as I watched the Commander piss his trousers and the photographers reload slide after slide into their cameras.

With a raise of my hand, I stopped the bloodbath and the Lwa returned to my side. The Commander surveyed his field, where over seventy of his men lay dead or dying. They were missing arms and legs, some were blistered by fire, or their skin flayed from their bodies. Cries and screams filled the air as men began to come out of hiding to offer medical assistance to the wounded.

I stood still as a stone, my eyes never betraying emotion, only staring into the soul of the Commander. The people of Dularge had watched from a distance, and their nighttime stories and nightmares had all come true. None of the tales of the Swamp Witch could compare to the violence they had witnessed tonight. None would ever forget, nor would their children or grandchildren.

I knew that the battle was over. No one would dare pursue me into the swamps now. I turned and walked back to my pirogue and poled away into the dusk.

†††

Tedré would occasionally bring me a newspaper from the city that had been left by one of the hundreds of gawkers and tourists that had come to Dularge in the wake of the battle. Andra Simmon's wrote with flourish and intensity as she described every fascinating moment of the battle, accompanied by spectacular photographs of the event. It was a marvelous success for Miss Simmon's, and it elevated her into New York society. It made her a wealthy woman.

But it brought me no wealth, only peace. No person of the swamps would bring an outsider to my home. No outsider who came alone ever survived long enough to make it to my meadow. Still, the sick and injured came to me to heal their bodies. Fortified by my companions and their Lwa, I was able to perform miraculous healings for my friends and neighbors. Now that they truly understood me, they took me under their wings, protecting me, as I would do for them.

If only life were that simple. Men have short memories, and time moves on.

The years passed with indifference. I was entirely content with my life. I did not feel the passing of years in my joints, memories, or stature. My skin sagged prodigiously about my chin and arms. My breasts had shrunken to tiny, wrinkled plums dangling from saggy bags of flesh. My feet were calloused and flat-footed from decades of barefoot use.

The ill were healed in exchange for fish or dry goods, whatever a local had in trade. The foolish got everything they asked for, and more in exchange for coin, which I had little use for, and hoarded in jars buried in the wet ground behind the house. The desperate would beg and I would negotiate harshly with them, demanding everything they had and more in exchange for a fantasy they desired. They were black hearts seeking wealth, fame, love, and power. They would leave with a promise of their desire, but it would be a double-edged sword that would slit their throats in time.

It was in this "time between" that I began to allow my Lwa to wander distances from me. They would venture into the swamps in search of sport, or to hunt, or to sit in solitude. The time had long past when either they or I would ever consider being apart from each other. We were separate, yet one. We were comfortable. Over time, one or more of my Lwa would be away for weeks or even months.

I also explored the boundaries of my own independent magic. Magic that was not tied to Maka, my parents or our Lwa. I discovered that I could bewitch objects to float or fly. I could send for fresh water from the stream 100 paces away to fill my wooden container in the house. I could fetch food or tools from great distances. I had even hunted alligator and wild birds with it. I used this sparingly, not wanting to be too reliant on magic, but needing to understand and expand my knowledge.

Although I could not lift myself, I discovered that I could take hold of an object and it could lift me. I was so much stronger than a mere mortal, but I was also old. I sat in a chair and lifted, swinging myself slowly in the air over the meadow. It was wonderful. I had branches lift me over canals and waterways in the bayou, allowing me access to parts of my environment previously too difficult to traverse. With my new freedom I felt years younger.

†††

I was immensely powerful, entirely magical, and full of cunning and guile, but I had everything I wanted in the witch's swamp. I had no desire to conquer lands far-off for wealth and glory.

I had lost count of the years, but by the reckoning of the people of Dularge, it was the year of 1950, and I would be 159 years on this earth. While in decades past I had relied on delivery of groceries and goods to me, I now sought out the noises and presence of society. Dularge was still just a place fishermen launched, but a canal had been build connecting Dularge to Dulac, allowing access in hours instead of days. Dulac was a proper town with schools, churches, bars, and canneries. It also had a medical clinic staffed one day a week from Houma. Medicine in the Bayou was news I welcomed and so I set out in my pirogue for Dulac.

Giant machines had carved out passageways between the lakes of the Bayou, expediting travel between regularly traveled places. While my home was still very remote and hidden, it took only an hour to reach the Falgout Canal which led to Dularge. I did not stop here but continued another five miles to Dulac. In the old days, by foot this was impassable. By pirogue you would paddle 30 miles south of Lake DeCade to Lake Merchant, then East to Caillou Lake then 30 miles north to Dularge. Now it was less than 10 miles in a straight line.

I had not been to Dulac in ages, not since my time with Maka. There were no landmarks I could recognize, although in the swamps, everything grows and changes swiftly. I did hope to see my old home, or the tavern, but these had long ago rotted into the swamp and had been replaced by modern steel buildings and manufactured homes. It was a dirty, filthy place, littered with trash and homeless. Telephone poles were being erected, bringing power to this backwater of the country. One company manufactured tin cans and ten companies canned fish in them.

I poled my way South along the bayou Dulac until I found the clinic. The sign noted that it was the Terrebonne Parish Clinic, Dulac, LA. Two men sat on the dock fishing, their pant-legs rolled up and their feet dangling in the warm water.

Both had a cold bottle of beer by their side, and it looked as if they cared not whether they caught a fish today.

I steered my pirogue to the dock and tied my small craft off, before nimbly stepping onto the dock. After many miles of standing and balancing in the boat, it took a moment for my land legs to adjust. I nodded to the men and stepped up the dock and onto dry ground. By my best estimation, I was not more than a few hundred yards from where my home and hospital had been, but now, instead of cypress and swamp, it was endless flat ground and fresh mowed grass as far as the eye could see.

I stepped onto the porch of the clinic and read the sign at the door. Doc Metarie, Physician, in peeling letters on the glass. I turned the knob and steeped into a small waiting room with three threadbare chairs. A fish-faced woman sat at a small desk, looking up at me through eyeglasses so thick her eyes looked several times larger than they likely were. "May I help you" she asked.

"I would like to see the doctor," said I.

"Do you have an appointment? His schedule is awfully full today," said she.

"I shall only be a minute" said I, "but it is most important that I see him".

She looked me over, seeing only a terribly old stranger with tattered clothing that looked like so many of the hermits that choose the Bayou life, only much older.

"Let me check his schedule", she said, and she stood and walked to the door of the clinic, opened it, and shouted "DOC, YOU AVAILABLE TO TALK TO THIS HERE

LADY"? One of the men fishing on the dock looked up and with irritation, stood, threw his pole to the ground, and stomped up the lawn to the porch. "Purty Beth", he said under his breath, "I told you my schedule was full today".

"She insists on seeing you, and she is awfully old. I was worried for her".

Doc Metarie eased past her and stood observing me. Neither of us said a word, but slowly his face and countenance changed. Eyes wide, and full of excitement he said, "you would be the Sorciére?"

"It is I" I said, "If you have a moment.."

"Please! Please!" He said excitedly, ushering me into his office. "Purty Beth, you get us some coffee and water, and then run to buy a package of those fancy cookies at the grocer. Git now!"

I sat in a large comfortable chair opposite his desk, and he hurriedly wheeled his chair from behind the desk to sit directly opposite of me. Although the chair was a reclining model, he sat on the front edge and leaned in close to me. I am so privileged to meet you. I have been coming here for nearly ten years to serve the people of the Parish and I have heard tales of your healing. I have witnessed amazing miracles of your cures and I have followed story after story of you. I would have visited long before now, but I felt that your privacy was most important to you. I am glad that you visited."

I was taken aback by this enthusiastic greeting. People either need me to heal them or give them something. This man's warmth and praise was without want or need, just for the joy of expression. It did my soul good.

Purty Beth brought in two mugs and a whole pot of black coffee, along with a small pitcher of water with two smaller glasses. She poured both the coffee and the water before excusing herself.

I drank the water in a single drought, for I was quite thirsty, but the coffee I savored. I had most often made chicory coffee from beans I harvested and ground in the locale of the meadow. To enjoy authentic coffee from an unchipped mug was a luxury I truly enjoyed. I spent a moment smiling and sipping, and the good doctor allowed me this time to savor.

I set down the mug on a doily seemingly set for the purpose, and I looked into the Doctors eyes. They were glassy and warm. They were open to me, and I could sense an honesty and childlike purity in him.

"Thank you for the kind welcome and high praise. I am a simple woman from the bayou, trained in healing by my parents and my partner, long gone, Maka. I have had much time to hone my craft, but I admit that it is a crude affair."

" You are too modest", he said. "I am aware of, and I believe in your magic, if I may call it that. I have read volumes of stories and accounts of your healing going back more than a century. I cannot begin to understand, but I do believe that you are a true healer with a gift. I am honored to share this time with you".

And the morning passed into afternoon. We exhausted the cookies, then the sandwiches that Purty Beth brought. We talked of herbs and plants, of infections and wounds. I shared remedies and he shared technology. He even showed me x-rays, allowing me to see inside an arm for the first time.

I was as mesmerized. As the sun began to set and the light faded in his office, I began to rise. It would not do to travel the bayou at night, for the hunters came out after dusk. The good doctor offered me a room in his rental home nearby and we walked down the lane towards his domicile, still talking of all things medical.

When we arrived, he showed me how to operate the shower and he fetched me a set of clothing belonging to his former wife. It was several times too large for me, but it was clean and folded like the day she left years ago. He made his good-byes and left me to my rest. I first went into the bathroom, looking at the clean tiles and the polished wooden floor. It was comfortable and welcoming. I stared for long minutes into the mirror above the sink. The wrinkles in my face were deep and many. It seemed only yesterday Maka and I were paddling in the bayou, and now so many years had passed since I had even looked upon his face. My hair was matted and windswept. For many years I had taken to keeping it close cropped to my skull as a utility way to keep the tangles and snarls from forming. Today it had grown wild and unkempt. Perhaps I would buy a pair of mercantile scissors tomorrow to cut it down to a manageable level. I turned on the water in the shower from the hot and cold knobs, as instructed, and felt the warmth creep up until it was just right. I stripped off my blouse and stepped under the water, feeling a chill run down my spine as the warm water poured over my wrinkled and knotted body. I used a bar of homemade soap to clean my hair first, watching the mud and dirt splatter on the walls and the floor of the shower is it cleaned a long-neglected scalp. I then worked the soap from my face to my toes, scrubbing myself long past the available hot water, and finishing up to a chilly cool deluge. The towels were thick, and store bought, unlike the flour sack cotton I used in my own home. I slept between white sheets of cotton, and I dreamed of new medicine the night through.

Morning found the smells of bacon grease and fresh coffee. I was revived and refreshed as I dressed in the clean, oversized clothing. I came into the dining room a new woman, and the appreciation of the good doctor was warming to me. He served up breakfast of eggs, potato's, bacon, and fresh coffee. We talked over the meal about diet and health. He shared thoughts from medical journals, and I shared the wisdom of Maka and my many years. The knowledge folded together harmoniously, and we found much to discuss.

Once at the clinic, there were a few patients already on the porch waiting admittance. While Purty Beth checked them in, the Doctor readied his two examination rooms. Purty Beth was well versed in prioritizing patients and those with the most need was always admitted first. I watched as Doc Metarie assessed a large fishhook that had pierced the arm of a fisherman. The hook was all of two inches long, and the barb was buried deep in the flesh. Doc Metarie felt around the hook and asked a few questions of the fisherman. While talking he had sponged the area liberally with disinfectant. Finally, without warning, he pushed the hook on through, the point erupting an inch farther along than the entry point. The man gave a squeal and blew out his breath through pursed lips, but the worst was done. The doctor clipped of either end of the hook with a set of pliers and then removed the remaining hook shaft. He sponged on more disinfectant, slapped a sterile compress over the punctures and sent the man back to his boat and nets.

I had seen hundreds of such fishhook injuries, and I could think of no better way to manage it, although I would have used manglier for pain, herbe à malo for inflammation. I distill my own alcohol for disinfecting, but if you can find eucalyptus leaves, they can disinfect as well.

Next was a pregnant woman who was early in her pregnancy. Doc was giving her a regular checkup and determined that everything was normal, giving her a clean bill of health. I asked if I may observe the patient, and the Doctor introduced me as a visiting colleague with expertise in rural healthcare. The woman looked me over head to toe, and was quite unsure of my credentials, but allowed me to place my hand, fingers splayed, on her gently swelling stomach. I held my other hand at her back. I gently massaged both, relaxing the woman, and both feeling and understanding the realities of this child inside. Firmly holding her back, I pressed with my right hand, rotating it clockwise around her belly. It was uncomfortable for her, and I could see her wince, but she was stoic as the women of the swamps were likely to be. She would not cry out, but she did look at me with mistrust and I quickly removed my hands from her. I smiled, with old yellow and black teeth that did nothing to foster confidence, and I stepped back for the doctor to check on her before releasing her.

Once we had the room to ourselves, with curiosity, Doc Metarie asked what I had done. The child was poorly positioned in the womb. Had growth continued, there was a chance that the cord would have cut off its airway. I had simply massaged it back into place. "But how did you know" he asked.

There is much to be said for touch and feel, but I have learned to sense and feel the child in the womb. You have an x-ray to inform you, I have my senses to inform me.

"Remarkable", he said.

The last patient was a man of early fifties. He had the hands of a fisherman, and the back of a much older man, beaten into a crooked posture from hours of long hard work. It was clear that this man, named Smith, was a good friend of Doc Metarie, and they chatted conversationally while the doctor did his assessment. The Doctor drew blood and labeled it to be sent to a laboratory, then asked Mr. Smith if he minded that I evaluate him. Mr. Smith had been watching me warily from the corner of his eye, but he knew not why I was present, nor had the Doctor introduced us. With hesitation, he placed his trust in the Doctor and agreed.

I already knew what the ailment was before I touched him. I could smell the cancer when he first walked into the clinic. I could feel its tendrils and fingers spreading out inside him. He was in late stages and would not long live with, or without treatment. Without bedside manner, I told him so.

The men exchanged glances. They had already had this discussion, but the Doctor wanted to know my ability, and the man likely felt some comfort in a second opinion, even if it were from an old woman with ill-fitting clothes.

The Doctor looked at me with deep feeling. "Is there anything you can do for him?" The short answer was yes, but there would be a steep price to pay. Cancers are a most devious illness. They effect both the healer and the Lwa when worked with. I generally just make the patient comfortable as they approach death rather than take the cancer into myself or my Lwa. My own magic could not do this, I would need my Lwa, and they would demand a steep price from the man.

"He is a friend of yours?" I asked. The Doctor shook his head yes.

"A very dear friend. If there is any hope for him, I would beg for it".

Mr. Smith was confused and trying to understand our conversation. He had long ago resigned to his slow, painful death by this cancer, and now Doc Metarie was pleading with this woman to save him. In his confusion, he asked for clarification.

Before Doc could answer I interrupted. "I am known as the Swamp Witch." I paused to let that sink in. His recognition took only a moment.

"I have heard of you, although I thought it a folk tale".

"Aye", I said. "I am the subject of many folk tales, many tall tales and many lies, but I am real, and I can cure what ails you, but there is a steep price, and I cannot tell you what it may be, because it is not me that will require payment."

I then began to tell my tale. A short version of Maka, and of Vodou and of the Lwa. Over centuries I have developed my own magic, but it is not enough to cure your cancer. For this, we must ask my Lwa. To heal you is to bring your cancer into both them and I. It is terribly painful and uncomfortable, but we survive it. I owe Doc Metarie a debt of friendship and I am willing to help where I can, but my Lwa, they will resist. If forced, they will require a payment from you, and you may not refuse. The payment may be greater than the cancer."

And there it was, out in the open. A decision for the man to make.

"May I think the night on it?" He asked.

"Certainly" says I, "but I must be leaving tomorrow, so you must make your mind".

Mr. Smith stood and held my hand in his own for long minutes. He looked into my eyes with crocodile tears and offered his thanks. He shook the Doctors hand, and he was gone.

The rest of the day was routine, with the Doctor and I both working side by side and learning from each other. I asked to borrow a pair of shears from his office, and there on the veranda of his office I cut away large lumps of matted hair until what remained was just an inch or so long. I swept up the hair and deposited it into the receptacle, and then joined the good doctor who was seated on the steps, looking out at the canal.

At days end, we made a meal of catfish and shrimp, and enjoyed a bottle of wine before saying our good nights. The Doctor resigned to his room, and I waited long minutes before stepping outside onto the lawn. I walked down the slope to the water edge and there I closed my eyes, raised the palms of my hands to the night sky and beckoned for my Lwa to come home.

†††

My Lwa were sluggish and lazy in their return. They had

long had free reign to roam where they would, and they were not in any rush to come back. That was until they were near enough to sense me, at which point they each swept me up in a joyous celebration of homecoming. Their spirits passed over, under and through me in affection. It was exactly what my body and spirit needed, and I shared my own affection with each of them.

When all settled, I sat in the tall grass and explained my friendship with the Doctor, his faith in me, and the request that we help Mr. Smith. My Lwa were in great spirits, and having not been worshipped in so long, were eager for the dance and song they knew I would provide. There was no small amount of speculation of what they might ask this man in return. It would be a glorious celebration. I went to bed that night optimistic for Mr. Smith and grateful to have my Lwa around me once again. We often do not know what we are missing until it returns.

Morning found me at the breakfast table across from the good doctor once again. I had slept well and found myself unusually cheerful, for I had been a dour and stoic woman for far too many years. I explained to Doc Metarie that my Lwa were agreeable to meet with Mr. Smith, but I still did not know what they would require of him.

Doc Metarie saw patients along during the day while I poled my pirogue out into the bayou in search of the items I would need for Mr. Smith. Despite the change of Dulac and the landmarks, I felt comfortable in choosing my path deep into the swamps, feeling a hominess that I had not felt in decades. I took my time poling the swamps and collecting my inventory. I returned near noon and fished an ancient coin from my purse to purchase a sandwich on the docks. They had no fresh water, but the man at the counter offered me a cola. I had no inkling what a cola was, but he assured me it would go well with the sandwich, and I took him for his word. With my feet dangling from the pier and the warm sunshine on my back, I tipped the bottle back, pouring a small dram of cola into my mouth. It tingled and fizzed. It was sugary sweet and altogether wonderful. I savored the cola as I had the coffee the day prior. The sandwich was a slice of bologna between two slices of homemade bread. There were slices of hard-boiled egg and dressings called mayonnaise and mustard. I died and went to heaven for sure.

I returned to Doc Metarie's office as the last patient left. Doc had Purty Beth close the shop and he bade her good night, leaving just the two of us in his operatory. The good doctor asked if he might be able to stay and witness the healing and I approved but told him that there was no way to tell if my Lwa would approve. We would wait and see.

I pulled a small table designed for surgical instruments to the center of the room and dumped the contents of my sack onto it. Feathers, bones, string and bits and pieces of colorful trash were all sorted and separated on the shiny stainless-steel top. I used the thread to string the feathers and trash into a makeshift headdress. The bones were of various animals of the swamp that I had collected. Last, I fetched a second small cotton sack closed with a knot and placed it on the table next to the bones. It writhed and moved as if possessed. Last, I stood and walked across the room to the doctors' instruments.

I fished around until I found a scalpel, and I placed this on the table as well.

At the appointed hour, Mr. Smith knocked on the door and Doc Metarie welcomed him inside. They wrapped each other into a warm embrace, hesitating to release each other, but anxious to move on. It was time to begin.

I carefully explained to both men that what would happen was very old magic. That my Lwa were very powerful beings who could either heal or harm Mr. Smith. Indeed, if provoked, they could harm the Doctor as well. The Lwa were a part of me, but I had little control over how what they would want in return for the healing. Both men agreed to the terms, and I instructed Doc Metarie to sit in a chair in the corner and not say or do anything unless asked to. To Mr. Smith I asked once again if he wanted to proceed, and with hesitation, he asked me to please try. I told him that he must not be alarmed by my dance or song, but that this was a gift to my Lwa. If he would be so kind as to dance with me, it would be a great compliment to my Lwa. I also told him there would be a sacrifice, and he should stand strong despite what he saw or heard. He nodded as he looked between me and Doc Metarie.

It was a warm, humid night, and Mr. Smith was sweating profusely. His body trembled with the excitement and fear of the moment. I unraveled the string of the headdress, and I placed it on my own head like a pauper's crown. I put a few of the small bones in each hand and I began to chant. It was a mumbling, guttural sound that came from deep in my throat. My hands shook with loose fists, causing the bones to rattle in the hollow of my fingers. My eyes were loosely closed, barely slits of black in a field of wrinkles. My feet shuffled at first, grazing the floor as I slowly walked around Mr. Smith. I could feel my Lwa stir. Their excitement palpable, but they remained patient, waiting for their moment. My chanting turned to song, low at first and building. My shuffling feet became dancing, and the bones rattled and drummed in my hands. I bid Mr. Smith to join me, and with uncommon grace, he waltzed around the room, arms holding an imaginary partner. My Iwa were indeed very pleased by this gesture. I motioned for Doc Metarie to join Mr. Smith in the waltz, and the pleasure of my Lwa was complete. Such absolute joy in the room, where sickness resided only moments before.

Using the scalpel, I sliced open the cotton sack and I fetched the small gopher snake inside. With a quick motion, I slit the snake head to tail and washed my arms in the warm, slippery blood. It was a warm blessing poured over the heads of my Lwa. They were in ecstasy as I blessed them, and they came forward into the room, rhythmically spinning and swirling about me and the men. Neither Mr. Smith or the good doctor could see my Lwa, but they felt the presence of something ethereal and were transfixed by our song and dance, as were my Lwa. I could sense them swaying back and forth as if in a trance, for the magic in this room was thick and heavy.

When my Lwa did appear, neither of the men were surprised or frightened. I extended a hand to the doctor, and he took it, the three of us in a festive dance of reverie. Laughter filled the small room, and we were all caught up in this joyous moment.

My Lwa were in rapture that these men would join in

the celebration, for in all the years, and all the selfish, greedy demands of people, none had joined the celebration before. My Lwa flew in and around the men. When they would pass through the men's bodies, the men would weep with joy, attempting to hold and hug these spirit beings.

Into the night we danced, until exhaustion overtook us all. We lay on the floor, basking in the afterglow of this beautiful moment. My Lwa were swirling overhead, like smoke whipped in the breeze. From my supine position, looking up into the spirits in the rafters, I explained to my Lwa that Mr. Smith had come to ask for a healing. I implored that he had come of his own volition, and that he deserved our consideration and care.

The spirits darted down from the ceiling, pouring themselves into Mr. Smith. They swam in and out of his body as he laughed and cried simultaneously. It was obvious that their presence was welcome and pleasurable to Mr. Smith, which is in sharp contrast to my expectations.

At length, Mr. Smith turned onto his side, and with a beatific smile, curled into a fetal position and slept soundly.

I asked my Iwa if they would cure Mr. Smith? If they would, what would his price be? What would my price be? The answer filled my spirit with love and pride for my Lwa. They had already cured Mr. Smith. They had deemed his dance to be worthy. They had seen inside of him and found him to be pure of heart and soul. They had been inside of Doc Metarie and saw their friendship, and the secret love they shared for each other since childhood. Their price had been paid over many years, and my Lwa were privileged to give them this small gift of life.

I stood on weak legs and looked down on the two men laying side by side on the floor, deep in slumber. I began cleaning the room of the feathers, and blood and sweat, until it looked once again like a surgery. I found light sheets to drape over them. Before I left, I spoke in the tongue of Maka, of the old Haitian and Creole. I wove a magic net of protection, love, and support over them. I stepped out into the beginning of dawn, and I spread my magic like a carpet over the entire town. The hatred, bigotry and exclusion that had tormented these good men, causing them to live a lie would be washed away by my magic. To each his own life, to each his own belief and choice. This was my message to Dulac.

I walked down the pier to my pirogue. The water inky black, with only a sliver of red and orange from the morning sky. I pushed my long pole into the mud of the canal, and pushed away from the dock, headed for home.

†††

The years that followed were not years of peace. An age of technology was blossoming. With technology came media, broadcasting, and television storytelling. It began as a science fiction story based on the tales of the Swamp Witch. These were not tales of healing and care, they were terrific stories of murder, bloodlust, and terror. Even in my remote, hidden world, these stories would arrive at my doorstep in the form of paperback books, or movie posters that patients wanted me to sign. I had forgotten how to read or write over a century ago. I had no use for their fan worship, or the attention that comes with it.

They came to me as bachelor parties, or spring break ghost hunters. They came as exorcists and televangelists. They came wearing black robes, claiming to be of New Orleans *Voodoo*, and wanting to apprentice to me. They came with incurable disease, psychological trauma, and desperation. The overgrown path up the meadow became a highway of people lining up to meet the Swamp Witch.

My patience thin, my anger seething and my willingness to help had long eroded. I used magic to bring the alligator and panther to my meadow, but then the hunters came with their guns and alcohol, killing everything they saw and leaving the carcasses to rot in the wind.

Yes, I had lost my patience with more than a few of them, and their corpses lined far off bayous where I had physically removed them. My magic was at a peak, and I could use it in nearly every form I wished, except to keep the hordes of *Witch Watchers* away.

Still, I tried to remain calm and placid for the few who were ill coming to seek me out for remedy. I used every ounce of my will to patiently turn away the tourist, or the gawker. On this morning, I was re-making my broom for sweeping of my domicile and porch. I sat on the steps of the porch with a strong hickory shaft, polished from more than a century of use and a bundle of dried, stiff meadow grasses for the brush. I was carefully braiding cordage out of the thicker, stronger grasses that grew at meadows edge. The broom brush was replaced twice monthly with fresh marsh grasses that seemed to work best after drying in the sun for a week or more. To make a very good broom you must first make cordage from the early shoots of meadow grass, when they are still tightly closed. You dry this grass for three days to eliminate moisture, then braid the grasses into a cord. You lay a portion of dried brush grasses at the end of the staff with the grass blades pointing upwards. You tie on one layer of grass with your cord, then a second, and a third, overlaying each layer to insure good coverage. When done, you pull the grasses downward into position firmly against the cords. You then wrap the grass with four coils of cord to hold the brush in place. Last, you soak the cordage, and the swelling of the grasses pulls the entire cord taught against the broom shaft.

With nimble fingers and centuries of experience, it takes no more than twenty minutes for me to complete the task with finished grasses at the ready. You first few sweeps are poor in performance, but as the brush begins to fray, the broom becomes far more efficient.

Sweeping is a meditation. I sweep slow, with shallow pulls of the brush to preserve its life. As I sweep, I hum to the rhythm of the brush. I sing low to my Lwa, telling them of their greatness and benevolence. I praise them for their gifts. I tease them with riddles and sarcasm, but I am always quick to beg forgiveness, for one never knows when sarcasm can be taken too far. From the distant parts of my mind, I could feel my Lwa great distances away. I could sense their pleasure and their happiness of my praise. Such was our sweeping ritual. My broom had become a part of my regular devotional to my Lwa. If I were to wait too long between sweepings, my

Lwa would grow impatient. We had developed a routine in a life that was previously irregular and chaotic. This routine was both comforting and disturbing. To grow to comfortable would always be met with a great disappointment, still we enjoyed this tranquil meditation while we could.

As time passed, I became more reliant on my magic, and less reliant on my old body. Besides the routine of having my water fetched for me and gathering herbs from the comfort of my porch by reaching far out with my mind, envisioning the ripe berries or most tender roots, and having them come to me. My magic was both functional helpmate and mindless entertainment.

Although I could magic objects to fly through the air, I was unable to magic myself from one place to another. I had tried holding on to rocks or sticks that I lifted, and this worked to an extent, but my frail hands could only hold on to a rock for so long before my fingers became stiff, and my arms strained.

I tried other objects as well. My rocking chair, which was comfortable, but not as swift as I had hoped. Taking from books of my childhood, I tried flying on an old hand-woven rag rug from my cottage, but it sagged in the middle and flapped in the wind. It was nothing like the fables of my youth. It was completely by chance that one day while sweeping and singing to my Lwa, that I sat gently upon the staff of the broomstick side saddle and willed it to rise. Rise it did, and I hovered a foot off the porch just as comfortable as you please. Yes, the staff was a bit uncomfortable on my bony backside, but it served as a much better option than the other objects I had magicked. It turned out to be very swift, quick in turns and easy to steer, with the brooms brush acting as a stabilizer, like the tail of a kite. I fashioned a new broomstick from a birch sapling, wrapping a thick layer of straw around its mid-section for comfort. It was completely unwieldy until I fashioned a new brush at the end. In the evenings, after long days of gathering herbs, cleaning house, and foraging for food, I would fly lazy circles around my bayou, looking down on the endless green carpet, the watery veins and the various animals that inhabited this glorious place. As my flights became bolder, I would cross large tracts of space at break-neck speeds, exhilarated by my newfound freedom. With my thin, white hair whipping in the wind behind me, I explored my small world.

Of course, a flying woman in the swamps was not natural, and under cover of mangrove and tucked in the tall cattails, I could not see everyone. Word spread that the Swamp Witch was out flying her broom, looking for children to snatch in the night for her supper. It scared off some good customers, but my regulars would delight in the knowledge that their protector and healer was above them, watching over them.

My dear friend Tendré had been such a confidante and helpmate to me for many years. With his old age and eventual death, this task was left to his oldest son, also named Tendré, and to the generations of Tendré that followed. More than friends, they became family. They were the only regular visitors to my domicile and were always welcome. They would bring mail, news, or caution. They came with canned foods, sweet treats, and an occasional bottle of wine, which we would split as we talked into the early morning hours. Tendré was my lifeline to the outer world, the only one I allowed. The only one I trusted.

Tendré knew of my Lwa, and although he feared them, he understood that they protected me, just as his parents protected him. Each generation of Tendré became more familiar with my Lwa, to the extent that they would talk about all manner of things long after I had fallen asleep for the night. The Lwa were fascinated with all things human, and Tendré with all things spiritual. My third Tendré was nicknamed Ten for simplicity, and at only twelve years of age, he asked to come study medicine and magic with me. At twenty, he was a skilled healer. At thirty he was caring for his entire communities of

Dularge and Dulac, leaving me with fewer local patients to treat, and opening the doors to more frequent visits from outsiders seeking a witch's magic, rather than healing.

A quiet and serious boy, Ten listened, asked intelligent questions, and never violated my trust, or that of the Lwa. When he passed his thirtieth year, the Lwa of Maka told me that it would possess Ten for its own. I had never given this thought, and before brazenly striking down the suggestion, I decided to contemplate it. The fact was, Maka's Lwa did not ask my permission, or Ten's. It made a statement, which concerned me greatly. Cautiously, I sought out Ten in Dularge where I told him of this turn of events.

Ten admitted to respecting and coveting my relationship with the Lwa, but also knew that this was a two-edged knife. It cut both ways. We discussed the compromises I made in life to accommodate the Lwa, and the benefits that they provided in healing and protection.

Ten stayed distant for several weeks, not wanting to tempt the Lwa. Frankly, the more he thought on it, the more afraid he became of losing his sense of self and identity. Lwa are brutal partners, and to invite them in was a dangerous undertaking. For them to possess you without your consent was even more alarming. Tendré did not wish to invite trouble onto himself, or his family.

As luck would have it, he never had to make that decision, for Ten was murdered in Houma while procuring medicines for his clinic in Dulac. His was not the first, for there had been three other similar incidents between Lafayette and Houma the previous month. Local police had one man in custody but released him on lack of evidence.

Ten's father was called, and he traveled North with his wife and daughter to collect the body of his son. They purchased a pine box coffin and placed him inside. They trucked him back home to Dularge in the back of Tendré's old 1941 truck. Not a tear was shed, nor would there be until Tendré, and his family had their vengeance.

I stood alongside the good people of Dularge as Tendré drove into the village. My tattered black satin dress, outdated and from a better time with the Major, standing out among the sweat-stained t-shirts of the menfolk, and simple cotton shifts of the ladies. The bayou was unusually quiet. There was no wind, few birds, and the usual sounds of the swamps were nearly silent as the old truck chugged its way across the rutted and always muddy track into town.

As the truck pulled to a stop in the center of town, the menfolk fetched the pine coffin and moved it onto two saw-horses that had been placed in the center of the village. The womenfolk surrounded Tendré's wife and daughter, holding and hugging them in a show of support and solidarity. No one approached Tendré, who had a seething anger haloed around him. He was volatile and near the breaking point, and it was palpable in the air. Only I dared to approach him. I wrapped my bony, thin arms around his rigid body, and I held him tight, he did not make a move to return the hug, and I did not expect him to. He was not here for me; I was here for him. In his ear I whispered, "I shall bring them to you, and you shall have your revenge". I could feel his body relax, if only a little, and I knew he felt a warmth and comfort in knowing I was there.

I stayed in Dularge, as a guest of Tendré's fishing partner. As is the tradition in these remote parts of Louisiana, when one dies, it is an honor to share stories about the departed as a community and family. Each day we gathered around the coffin, still in the middle of the village, and we feasted, danced, and played lively music that was not designed to bolster our spirits, but the spirit of the departed Ten. My four Lwa basked in this song and dance but remained unusually restrained. I took notice of Maka's Lwa, who radiated a peculiar emotion, but one I could not directly associate with. Most important, we shared storied of Ten's short life. Great care was made to not allow emotion to bring negativity or revenge to these stories. As much as it was on everyone mind, it was important to keep these stories about goodness, light, and better times. This is how we would remember Ten.

†††

When it comes to revenge, I was a consummate professional. I was without conscience, and without fear. I had no timeline or worry about my own mortality. I was eternal, powerful, and damning. There would be nothing that would, or could, stand between me and my mission.

Upon returning to my domicile in the bayou, I did not rest or eat. In the same tattered satin dress I had worn for days, I sat astride my traveling broom, and I rose into the skies, hell-bent for Houma. A dark visage astride a homemade broom that would become iconic hereafter.

I set my feet on firm ground in front of the Parish

constables office. With my broom in hand, I walked up the cement and stone steps and into the building, demanding the watch captain to know the identity of the man questioned for the murder of Tendré Olefant. The watch commander stared in wonder at me, a frail, haggard woman, hair close cropped to a bony skull, an ancient dress from a different time and place. No doubt he thought me insane.

"Miss", he said, with amusement in his voice, "can I have an officer help you find your home?"

I had not the patience or temperament to play his game, so I reached over his counter, took him by the collar and drug him over, spilling papers and his coffee in the process. I lifted him clear of the floor and demanded and answer.

If I were a spectator, I surely would have laughed out loud at the surprise of the officer. Not only at my action, but that a woman of my age and condition could achieve this feat. But I was not a spectator, I was a dangerous Sorcière, and my full power became apparent as the officer summed up what his re-action should be. Wisely, he chose to show his hands, and ask me politely to let him down, he would be happy to help me.

That was the moment two uniformed officers rushed through the office door, guns drawn at the commotion and apparent threat. Seeing an old lady, holding their brother officer aloft, startled them for a moment. I lowered the officers' feet to the floor, and I brushed his suit jacket lightly. I turned to the two still holding their guns and swept the small artillery into dust with a wave of my hand.

"It is the Swamp Witch", said the deep voice of a calm man, entering the room from another of the several doors leading in and out of the lobby. "Please, would you please follow me to my office", said he. I followed, to the surprise of the other three in the room.

"Please, have a seat", said the tall man. He was slightly gray of hair, a large handlebar mustache and built like a man who worked for a living. He had a distant familiarity about him, although I could not place it. "My name is Field Inspector Tone Dunstill. My Great Uncle was a Major in the Union Army. Perhaps you would remember him?"

It is very difficult to surprise me. Moreso to stop my heart from beating in my chest. My mouth agape and my eyes wide, I simply said "My Major Dunston"?

With a comforting smile, he said, "Yes, your Major Dunstill". He left a large body of writing about his time after the war, much of it related to you, although it stops when he decided to take you to Cuba. I learned of the arrests in Atchafalaya, but no more is written about him thereafter. Perhaps you could fill in the story for me?"

I sat quite still for long minutes. Tone Dunstill poured me a cup of water from the pitcher on his desk, and I sipped it slowly, searching for the words. When I looked up into his eyes, they were as watery and red as my own, for he had grown up with stories of his Great Uncle, the Swamp Witch, and their love, since childhood. He had written about it exhaustively in University and had coveted the Majors writing to this day.

Slowly at first, then with increased enthusiasm, I told the entire story of the Major and I, from start to finish. He sat, all attention on the story, smiling and even laughing as I filled in parts he had not known. I left out the parts admitting my guilt to the murder of officers in the train car, and those on board the salvage boat, and the exclusions were obvious, but not challenged. When I told him of waking next to the Majors still, dead body, his face clouded, and I could see the same steel and resolve that the Major embodied. I finished my story with the explosion of the tramp steamer, and the eternal resting place of the Major.

For long moments there was only the ticking of the cheap Timex wall clock. Tone rose from his chair, took my hand, and assisted me to my feet. "Let's go get a bite to eat at the diner, and I will tell you all I know of Tendré".

As we left Tone's office, a roomful of wary and curious police officers was in the lobby waiting to see what would happen. Tone gently brushed them aside and held the front door for me. We walked down the street, catching the eye of many onlookers, and entered a small diner that Tone favored.

Desi was the name on the tag of our server, and she could match me scowl for scowl on my worst day. So sour was she, that even I was amused, but under that crust was a heart of gold, I could feel it and I winked at her as she seated us in a booth at the far end of the room.

We sat quiet while Desi poured hot coffee and fetched two ice waters. Tone ordered a club sandwich for each of us, with a side of potato salad, and I thanks him, for I had never eaten in a place like this and knew not what to do, or what to get.

Tone started our conversation with a condolence to myself and to the Olefant family, which I appreciated and thanked him for. He noted that in his research of the Swamp Witch over his lifetime, the Olefant family was often mentioned as respectful and honorable people. What happened was a tragedy, and he was personally investigating it.

"Before I go on, I need to know what your intentions are with the information I give you".

I did not hesitate to answer, " I will exact revenge on behalf of myself, of Ten, of the Olefant family and of the communities of Dulac and Dularge which he served".

It was not the answer Tone wanted, but it was the one he expected. "I am bound by the law to prevent anyone from interfering with my investigation or taking the law into their own hands. You are putting me in a very uncomfortable position."

I acknowledged the fact but offered that if he had done his research thoroughly on who I was, and what I was capable of, the best thing he could do for all concerned would be to turn his suspect over to me".

"We were unable to gather any evidence on this young man, but I feel he knows more than he is telling. I will strike a bargain with you. You and I will investigate this together. I will lead, and you may witness. If I ask for your assistance, you may participate, but otherwise, you may not incite any violence toward any person during this investigation."

My response, again, was not to his liking, but exactly to his fear. I welcome you to investigate alongside of me. You may ask your questions, but if any person refuses to cooperate, I will use my will, my magic, and my Lwa to extract the information we need."

This is where Tone thought the discussion would go,

and he knew that this was his best chance to avoid full-scale vengeance. "There is one more thing," he said. I want for the District Attorney to join us. This will eliminate any chance for persons to claim I let you run roughshod over the investigation, and she has an iron will to match your own. The two of you will become best of friends or will fight it out in the streets. I would not lay odds on either of you coming out on top in that brawl."

I smiled. A whole face smile that wrinkled my cheeks and squinted my eyes. How foreign it felt! How long had it been since I felt true humor and happiness. Decades? I felt it in my bones that this joining of good people together to find the truth would provide the best result. I also knew in my heart that regardless of what kind words were said today, tomorrow I would deliver the murderer to Tendré. He deserved his revenge.

†††

Jane Doucet was another familiar face. Fortunately, she did not know her family history, and she would never know that Coy Doucet was distant family to her. Families were built, and stayed, in Louisiana. Family names were passed down, and the branches of the family tree spread wide.

Jane Doucet was indeed a brassy spitfire. She had been the Louisiana District Attorney for better than twelve of her forty-three years. During that time, she had taken on gangs, organized crime, murderers, rapists, and every deviant criminal to come along. Her conviction rate was enviable, and she gave no quarter to anyone who did not deserve it. I liked her the minute we met. Although I was old and frail, she shook my hand with a firmness that was both solid yet yielding. She looked right into my eyes when she spoke and she did not mention, or even act alarmed at my dress or the homemade broom I carried with me. Tone told her that he needed her, he introduced me as a friend, and that was good enough for Jane Doucet.

It was only when Tone mentioned that I was the famed *Swamp Witch* that Jane Doucet broke her steady gaze. She roundly turned to Tone and asked, "what in God's name did you call her?".

"She is the Swap Witch, in the flesh."

Jane turned to me with curious caution. "The Swamp Witch, as in the mythical sorcerer that lives west of Dularge?"

"The very same."

Knowing that Tone was not known for his sense of humor, Jane looked me up and down, twice. "Are you the Swamp Witch"? she inquired.

"I am," I replied matter of fact.

Jane looked at Tone, then again at me. " I don't know that I believe in the Swamp Witch," she said.

"It does not matter if you believe or not," I offered. "I come here as a favor to Tone, and I will honor our agreement."

Jane processed all of this quickly and efficiently.

Well, she started, what are we here to discuss?

†††

Laney Parsons was from a good family. They ran a small farm nearby and were known and liked by just about everyone. Unfortunately, Laney did not share his family's respect. He was a bad seed, through and through. He had dragged the family name through the mud since grade school, but the people of the community saw him for what he was and did not hold it against his family. He was just Laney.

As Tone parked his black cruiser in front of Laney's single-wide trailer, Laney was sitting in a tattered folding chair, no shirt, or shoes, smoking a cigarette and drinking straight from the bottle of Beam. He smirked and slouched deeper in the chair as Tone and Jane exited the front seat. I, as agreed, would stay in the car unless I was needed. I could hear fine, so I would not show my teeth unless necessary.

"Laney", began Tone, " This here is District Attorney Jane Doucet.

"Howdy Jane, "said Laney. "Always good to see you."

Jane scowled and held her words. "Laney, we know you was involved in the death of Tendré Oliphant. We can't pin it on you now, but you would be doing yourself a favor to tell us what happened and who else was involved."

Laney spat on the ground at Tones feet. "I got nothing to say to you. You ain't got no evidence, you ain't got no leads and you ain't got nothin to hold over my head" he said with a buck-toothed grin.

"That's not exactly true Laney," said a smiling Jane Doucet. "We have an ace up our sleeve. If you don't want us using it, you should share what you know right now."

Laney stood up from his chair, flicked his cigarette at the DA's chest and turned to walk into his trailer.

"Stop right there", I shouted as I exited the car. "You and I have something to discuss Laney Parsons."

Laney turned to see a haggard old crazy woman walking

towards him. He scoffed and stood defiantly as I came ahead. Jane was smiling, but Tone was on high alert. "Please" was all he said to me. I nodded and stood face to face with the cocky Laney Parsons.

"You will tell me what we want to know, I said, entwining my words with magic to compel an answer. Laney started to speak but the words coming out of his mouth were not the ones he intended. "I was there, but it was the Nesbitt brothers that killed that man. We just intended to take his money, but he fought back, saying it was for medicine for his clinic. We all know medicine is expensive, and we figger we got us a good deal of money comin. Still, he fought us, and Bobby Nesbit shoved a shank into his belly and Billy hammered him with fists until he didn't move no more. We split the cash three ways and I ain't seen hide nor hair of those Nesbit boys since."

I turned to Tone, and he mouthed a thank you. Tone handcuffed the boy and led him back to the cruiser. Jane Doucet turned to me and looked at me very curiously. "Why did he tell you that," she asked?

"Because I told him too," was my response, and I walked back to the car, leaving her standing alone.

I did not worry about Laney Parsons. He was in jail and would keep until I needed him. Over pie and coffee, Tone, Jane, and I discussed where to find the Nesbit brothers, and what they were likely to do when we found them. "They are tough boys that run with a tough gang", said Jane. They all hang out at the roadhouse up Thibodaux way."

"I know the place, and I know the crowd," says Tone. "We

aren't likely to get the Nesbit's without having to tackle a dozen of their mob."

"A dozen is not so many," I offered. Tone scowled and Jane just stared at me for a long time. She was not a believer in magic, but before the day was over, she would know me for who I was.

The drive north on Park Avenue to the Roadhouse was just under fifteen miles, and we drove in silence. I hummed softly to my Lwa. They sensed excitement ahead and needed calming.

We pulled off the paved road and onto the dirt lot that served for parking at the Roadhouse. It was your typical biker bar. A handful of motorbikes out front, a few beat up trucks and one clean Lincoln Continental that likely belonged to the owner. The music was too loud, the lights too dim and the smell was of piss, vomit, and alcohol. All of this was foreign to me, and it felt like the evil it was.

As we walked in, it was obvious that Tone was known as the *Law*. Jane looked entirely out of place in her black skirt and white blouse, and I, the wrinkled old hag was a mystery. We made quite an impression as we stepped inside and surveyed the assortment of characters.

I could have magicked the Nesbit's to me, but respected Tones request and followed his lead. He wove through unmoving bodies across the floor, each person steeling themselves to the floor, in a not so delicate way of reminding Tone that he was unwelcome here. There would be no easy navigation of the bar.

The owner came from the back room, waving us over, but

we ignored him. He knew this was trouble, and he wanted to minimize damage to his bar, and stay on the good side of the law. When he recognized the District Attorney as one of us, his confidence evaporated, he knew he would be shut down for sure.

Tone spotted the Nesbit's, who made no move to run. They leaned against the bar, sipping warm beer, and acting the cock of the walk. Tone walked right up, dropped two set of handcuffs on the bar and said, "Bobby and Billy Nesbit, you are both under arrest, put them on." Bobby Nesbit brought his left hand from behind his back, the glint of his Bowie Knife glinting off the dim bar lighting. Tone noted it and took a step back, not in fear, but to open room to work. Jane had not seen the knife and she walked up alongside Tone, who used his left arm to bar her advance and shove her back into the crowd.

"You don't want to do this", said Tone. "I am the Law, and you are digging your hole deeper."

Bobby Nesbit brought the knife up and began cleaning the grease and dirt from under a fingernail. He recklessly ran the point up under the nail and he withdrew his bloody finger, shaking his hand and yelping like a beat pup. This drew laughter from the bar patrons, and even a smile from Billy Nesbit, who now held his right hand at his belt, behind his work jacket. Tone knew what was in that hand, and he reached for his service revolver, drawing a bead on Billy, and looking at Bobby.

With things escalated, everyone in the bar scattered. Now it was just the Nesbit brothers, Tone, gun in hand, Jane backing up her officer with a small service revolver of her own, and me, an old lady in a tattered, ancient black dress.

I stepped forward to face the brothers. Jane tried to stop me, but Tone did not. "You boys do what the constable says. I would hate for this to get out of hand before the family of Tendré Oliphant has their say."

Billy slid his hand from his belt, now holding a nickel-plated revolver down by his side, casual and relaxed. "So, this is 'bout that guy we robbed?" says Billy.

"No", said I. "This is about the man you killed."

"We just cut him and beat him a little. We didn't kill no one. You couldn't prove it if we did, we was alone."

The thought hit Billy and Bobby at the same time. They were not alone. Laney had been with them. That squirrely fink could not keep his mouth shut.

"Billy raised his gun and his arm dissolved in a spray of red. Bobby wasted no time figuring out who hurt his brother, or how, he stabbed forward with his Bowie, and as the knife touched the satin of my skirt, the blade and his arm dissolved with it. No mess, no pain, no worry.

All was still as a church in the bar. As Bobby and Billy Nesbit tried to wrap their minds around their new situation, I turned to face the others. "Who among you claim to be the friend and associates of these two boys", said I.

A half dozen tattooed, rough men stepped forward. They were brothers in bond and would not betray their brothers or their club. As Tone shouted "NO", I waved a hand, and each of the men before me lost their right arm to the elbow. For a moment there was silence, then I allowed the pain to force its way into every mind. It was absolute pandemonium. Some men fell to the floor, others ran out into the street. Tone shook his head at me, and Jane stood staring, dumbfounded.

Long after the Nesbit's were in their cell, across the hall from Laney; Tone, Jane and I sat in his office, a bottle of bourbon and three glasses between us. Jane had not said a word since the bar, and now she struggled with the right words to say. I held up my hand, and I gave her an abbreviated version of my life to this moment. Unable to grasp the truth, she shook her head and tried to rationalize what had happened. This would be difficult, as it was not a rational event.

Tone spoke up, first thanking me for stepping in when I did, and second to chastise me for my poor judgement. "You could have been hurt. You could have died" he said. In all of this, Tone Dunstill was worried about me more than himself. I softened to the thought of how proud the Major would be of his kin.

"Please think of it this way," I exclaimed. "I could have done much worse."

"I know, and that is what worries me", said he. "Was this the work of your Lwa? Was it done without your consent?"

"Oh no, Tone. I kept my Lwa subdued and took care of this little fracas myself."

"You did this with your own magic?" he asked" "What is the difference between what you can do, and what your Lwa can do?"

"I have a conscience and think about consequence. My Lwa are spirits that cannot be controlled or contained. Were they to be let loose, no speck of dust would remain of the bar, or its patrons. My Lwa and I occupy a very delicate understanding. One that can be rent open and destroyed with the slightest provocation. My Lwa trust me to use my best judgment regarding whether they are needed, or not. Still, I must warn you that there is one that I will not control for much longer. It was determined to be bound to Ten, to become part of him. When Ten was murdered, this Lwa lost its opportunity to bond with the boy. For this, I believe much blood will be spilled. It is not for me to say who or when, but I fear it is coming.

Tone sat in silence and contemplated his empty glass, Jane sat unmoving, unsure what to believe, or how to use it.

†††

Late in the night, long after Tone and Jane had left for their respective homes. Long after respectable restaurants and social halls had closed, I sat astride my broom and let out for the Roadhouse.

The parking lot was full to overflowing. News had spread, and everyone wanted to know what had happened. There were also news vans and city gawkers present. It had become an event. The owner, who should have been overjoyed at this boon to his business, fretted over potential political fallout from the unusual day. He had paid the proper authorities, but he knew that the story was much bigger than his small payments.

I left my broom leaning against the building and like a character from a western movie, I stepped through Bat-wing doors and into the bar. Slowly, the mood shifted as people saw I was inside, and they spoke in hushed voices to their friends and bar neighbors until only the jukebox, with it screeching whining country western music remained. I wished it silent, and the 45rpm disc slowed to a stop, slurring the crooners last words as it died out.

I stepped into the room barefooted, as was my preference. I had wrapped my head in a black cotton scarf to compliment my tattered black ensemble. I walked in and out of the patrons, who quickly moved aside. As I reached the center of the room, I raised my arms gracefully and began to dance, slowly, sensuously. Even in my advanced years, my dance stirred the loins of the men and wetted the thighs of the women. I danced of sex and of sensuality as bodies began to move around me. Ever so slightly following my movements. I began to sing a song of Saint Domingue, in an ancient Haitian. I told tales of Bondýe and the Lwa. Of slavery and escape, of Maka and I. Bodies were now moving in synchronicity with my own. I could feel my four Lwa breathing in our dance, reveling in my song. I sang of Tendrè the grandfather, of Tendrè the father and of Ten the son. My pitch climbing, my voice growing louder, my intensity elevating and my Lwa now in a state of frenzy.

As one they rushed from my body, slicing, skewing, and destroying everything in their path. It was a tornado of blood and wood and glass swirling around me. Screams and cries lasting only a moment, and then it was just the sound of the wind.

I stepped from the bar into the starry night, with a full moon as audience. I collected my broom and set off for

Houma, the roadhouse dissolving into dust in my wake, leaving no trace that it, or the patrons ever existed.

†††

I arrived at the constables' offices and jail at 5am. I walked through the lobby, past the guards and orderlies who neither saw nor sensed my presence. It took several moments to find the cells that held Laney Parsons and Bobby and Billy Nesbit. I tore the cell doors from their hinges, swept up the three men with magic, and I blew the rear wall from the jail with a mere thought. I rose into the early dawn on my broom, with three men dangling from unseen tethers. We flew fast and furious south to Dularge.

Early morning is a time of activity in a fishing town. By daybreak, boats had already been offshore and returned. Men were busy at the docks with the nights catch, separating prawn from shrimp, from crab and any other sea life they managed to capture in their nets. The long-line fishermen were unloading yellowfin tuna, dolphin, swordfish, and sharks that had swallowed their hooks.

News spread quickly, and every man abandoned their work to rush to town center. In the very place where Ten had been days before, now stood three scared men and an old hag of a Swamp Witch.

Tendré himself ran up to greet me, taking hold of me tightly, hugging me close. "Thank you, my witch, thank you for bringing me my revenge. Thank you". This was followed by a rousing cheer from the assembled. Once again, the Sorciére had shown her care for the community. Once again, she had proven her kind heart and faithful service.

Tendre faced the three men before us. He demanded that these men confess before the whole village. When none of the three volunteered, I compelled Laney to be the first. Without the ability to hold his words, Laney told the tale of the robbery, stabbing and beating that took the life of young Ten. When he was done, Tendré slid his fisherman's fillet knife from his belt scabbard, and swiftly swept upwards. A cut so precise and delicate that the blood did not begin until Laney brought his hands to his throat, after which the blood flowed with each beat of his dying heart.

Seeing this, the Nesbit Brothers cried and blubbered like babies, but each was compelled, and each would succumb to Tendré's blade. Three bodies, laying in the Louisiana mud and dust, each bleeding out as a sacrifice to Tendre, the Oliphant family, to me and to my Lwa.

Tendré walked to a water trough and cleaned his hands, then returned to his domicile to grieve in private. The community came together as before, removing bodies to a pirogue to be hauled into the swamps, shoveling up the blood left behind and disposing of every scrap of evidence that would tell the tale.

It would be nearly an hour later that Tone and Jane arrived to Dularge in the black sedan. All seemed a normal day, with the fish vendors finished icing their catch for the journey North to Baton Rouge, or East to New Orleans. Tone surveyed the village and found no obvious evidence that the witch or the men had been here, but he could see the grim satisfaction of the locals. He could feel the vindication coming off them in waves.

Tone went to the domicile of Tendré. He knocked, hat in hand, and offered his condolence to Tendré when he answered the door. He asked a few questions and got the expected answers. Direct questions about the witch or the men were unanswered. Tendré would neither admit nor deny, leaving Tone to find evidence elsewhere.

It had been many years since Tone had poled a pirogue, and Jane had never even been in one. They hired a guide to take them to my domicile, and hours later, they were stepping onto my dock. Within twenty minutes they were seated at my kitchen table, where I served up supper of wild harvested wild lettuce, sorrel, and greenbrier, chantarelle mushrooms, Chickasaw plums, and roasted alligator tail.

It was the same table that served as my surgery over centuries. Under the cotton sheet that served as my tablecloth were the stains of the blood of criminals and honest men. The same where I birthed children, treated wounds and illness. Where some were saved, and some would die. This history was hidden under the thinnest slip of old white cotton.

We never discussed the Roadhouse.

What we did discuss was leaving this small world for a larger one. Was my healing for one person at a time, or could I heal whole communities, whole nations? I had an obligation and a duty to use my magic for good.

I argued that I had seen too little good. That my best efforts to use magic as a tool for healing was turned into greed or ascendent violence. Where I went, people died. My code was not the code of civilization. It was born of my ignorance and selfishness. Of my desire to be left alone, and the refusal of the world to allow it.

The conversation did not sway me, but it influenced my thinking. I was just one woman. A simple healer from a remote place. Were there other like me in the world? Could they guide my magic and make me a useful tool for humanity?

†††

Moring found Tone and Jane sleeping side by side in my bed, albeit fully clothed. An innocent sharing of space and comfort. Tone, with his arm draped over Jane in a protective way. Jane in a dreamless, safe sleep. I almost wanted to be here when they woke and found themselves wrapped in each other, but I had places to be.

I gathered a few personal possessions, bundled in a knotted scarf, and I boarded my broom. I would spend weeks around the southern states of Mississippi, Alabama, Tennessee, the Carolinas and eventually found myself at the foot of Florida. I wandered in a swamp called the *Everglades*. It was a beautiful area of bayou and cypress, entirely unlike my Dularge home, but entirely similar. It was in the Everglades that I began to assess the great charity and love I had witnessed over the last several months. I also saw firsthand the evils of bigotry, division, violence, and fear.

What was I here for? Why did I have Lwa that preserved me and granted me this immortality. Why did I own this magic? Why not others who were more prepared to take advantage of the gifts? I was a simple woman of the Bayou, not a hero from the big city.

I resolved that I was justified in my ownership of everything I embodied. I had given all I could to those who came to me injured, weak and desperate. I had been fair when others sought to gain advantage, I had served as the judge, jury, and executioner to those would harm me, or harm those I loved. It was a simple justice, but it was mine, and I owned it.

I knew that from Temmy Rowan to Mr. Smith, my actions had been unselfish and justified. I had learned independence from my Lwa, and I had taught them restraint and obedience. I owned my body and spirit. I allowed my Lwa to exist within me. They served at my bidding, and when turned loose, they unleashed a mighty vengeance on those who would harm us.

Yes, I was justified.

Now I had to determine if it were simply enough to remain

in my bayou home. To wait for more of the same to come to me, or should I take my justice outside into the world? Would I find peace, or futility?

I determined to go on a mission. A single flight that would take me far from my home and my comfort. Away from friends and those who would protect me. A journey into the unknown for the sake of justified vigilantism. It was time for me to venture outside, and into the world.

†††

I did not attempt to fly to Saint Domingue in a single trip. My broom carried me from the Everglades to Key West, a series of small Islands a few hours flight south. From there it was a long crossing of the Caribbean to Havana.

Havana! This was a place to live. Such life and love rooted in poverty and family. I would stay months in Havana city, healing and learning the people and language. I was open with both my magic and my Lwa, which was welcome and celebrated here. On the recommendation of locals, I would stop to visit friends, family or the infirm in Matanzas, Santa Clara, Camaguey, Holguin, and the far south of Guantanamo. The many smaller villages along the way would host me for a night or a week. I would learn the language and talk deep into the night about all manner of life and magic.

There was no Vodou in Cuba, save a few practitioners of something that resembled Vodou, but it was not a Vodou that I recognized. It was a weak and watered down devotion, void of any magic, or Lwa connection. It was recital of prayers, and singing of songs that did not encourage or attract Lwa.

It was good people wanting to believe in something, but not believing in anything enough to matter.

In Camaguey, I met a woman that was a kindred spirit. For three days we danced, sang, and offered sacrifices. My own Lwa reaching far and wide for any trace of Bondýe or Lwa, but we found that too many years had passed. Too few songs over the centuries. I was confused. I had thought the Lwa existed in a spirit world everywhere, but it seemed that they attach to people and places, and are hesitant to move, perhaps for fear of leaving what they knew, for an unknown. It would seem people and spirits have more in common than I had assumed.

Another long crossing and I was in Jamaica. This was a land with a rich Vodou heritage, and my visit was predicted by the local Onguan and Manbo, who held a formal ceremony for my arrival. On my first night, we feasted and danced on the beach of Negril. With a warm welcome from our fellow Vodou, I was shown some of the rudimentary magic that these people possessed. It was feeble, but in it, they were proud and assure. I was given a glimpse of an elders Lwa. It was a dim visage that had come forward fearfully, coaxed out by the song and dance. It stayed but a moment, retreating into the shadows.

After much food and drink, my hosts asked me about my magic, and whether I had witnessed an Lwa. I had become aware that magic was a rare thing to behold in Vodou, and that Lwa did not reside inside of the Onguan or Manbo, they were spirits loose and seeking connection, but fearful of the commitment.

I stood and approached the fire. I bowed low to the assembled Vodou congregation, and I began to tell them the story of Makindal, and of Maka. These stories had been all but lost to antiquity, and each person sat in rapt attention. As I spoke of Maka, I began to writhe and move. Like a snake's tongue flickering, or a stork's wings on takeoff, I moved with sinuous grace. I spoke of the Petra and Rada spirits that resided in us, and there was a murmur of surprise that we allowed a possession, which was forbidden, and that the Lwa chose to reside within us, which was not of the norm. I could sense the Lwa in the shadows listening with the same intensity as the devoted. Each learning a new way, a new magic.

I spoke of our healing, and of the assistance our Lwa provided, avoiding the parts that were unsavory, or the people who came to us with greed and desire. I spoke of calling Lwa for my parents. A loud guffaw was heard and the Oungan stopped the ceremony, for I was now making light of a very serious belief of these people. No one can call an Lwa. No Lwa would reside in a single human. This was blasphemy.

I was tolerant, for they had not witnessed any proof. I asked for order and begged their attention. I warned all to sit quietly and observe, but not interfere.

With all seated and quiet. I began my dance. I sang of the benevolence and power of my Lwa. Of its generosity and help though centuries. I sang of Maka and my parents, and of our bond in both body and spirit. I felt my Lwa stir, and seep out of the pores of my skin, prickling my arms with gooseflesh. It was faint as smoke in the beginning, but as my Lwa came into their prominence and began to form, rapid talk and whimpering could be heard among the gathered. I sang louder, of the goodness in Lwa, and that all should celebrate the power and magic they give to us. Now my Lwa were in full form, tall as trees and swaying to the rhythm of my dance and song. Several people stood and ran, afraid of the spirits within me, but most stared in awe. I had not one Lwa within me, but four. My Lwa began to send out tendrils of welcome and love to the adherents of Vodou. These were their people. They invited each to joining the song and the dance, and slowly, each joined us until there was laughter, song and dance that drew the Jamaican Lwa from the shadows to celebrate with their people.

The stars seemed brighter that night. The moon more radiant. The people more appreciative and the Lwa completely under the spell of their adoring congregation. Long after I left, the Vodou of Jamaica would find new relationships with their Lwa, and new magic in their hearts.

†††

Dame Marie is a small coastal village in Haiti. Long the target of hurricanes and in the deepest pit of poverty, Dame Mari is resolved to exist. From the moment I touched down, the children of this small village swarmed me for pennies, food, or water. My heart melted in this desperation, and I held my hands, palms out, to show that I had none. They were not deterred. Desperation demands the victim to beg. To plead for help, even when none is available.

I asked the children to gather wood for a large fire. As they gathered, the mothers and fathers came, curious why their children were doing this. They brought driftwood from the beach, old broken chairs and scrap that were discarded in the streets. There was no pride in community here. No clean homes or cheerful flowers. This is where dreams came to die, and all hope with it.

With the fire roaring, and coals beginning to form, I stood on the beach and began my dance and song to my Lwa. The children, in a display of absolute joy, came and danced with me. I begged the parents and adults to come, and they did. There was so little cause for celebration in their lives, that this one moment of happiness was grasped by all. My Lwa were overjoyed at the celebration of the people. A community with nothing, laughing and singing for the simple joy of it. I sent my Lwa into the deep water offshore. Moments later, I netted my fingers together and reached as if to dip into the ocean. When I threw my hands shoreward, hundreds of fish came forth from the water, slapping and flopping on shore. The community rushed to play the game of catching the slippery fish, tossing them into the coals to roast. From the local village well, meager as it was, I coaxed an abundance of fresh water, which was fished out bucket by bucket to fill earthen urns. Within minutes, the community was peeling flesh from the bones of the fish and drinking fresh water. It was the only feast these children had known, and only a memory to the adults, who had rarely had a full belly.

My Lwa came ashore with boats, long sunk in the shallows, and with driftwood to patch them. It was our hope that these gifts would be used to help this small community exist, if not prosper.

Bellies full and sated, the people clung to my arms and

legs to keep me forever. A goddess of the air and sea, come to save them.

But leave I did, encountering the same desperation and poverty in Aquin, Marouane and worst of all Port Au Prince. The slums overflowing with illness and starvation. I stayed for months without seeming to dent the need. Haiti is dotted with small Ounfò, each but a small gathering place for a handful of remaining adherents. Catholicism brought money and riches to the politicians, who in turn nearly decimated Vodou in the 1940's. Today, it seems to be a lost belief. Its Lwa faded into memory, for we found few in our searches.

I sent messengers on to the Dominican Republic, which was formerly known as Saint Domingue, the home of Makandal and Maka in the time before. My messengers sought assistance from my Vodou brothers and sisters, but none came. I served as a bandage, a patch on the souls of the poor and desperate. The more poverty I encountered, the angrier I became. How could Bondýe and the Lwa abandon these people? With such power, they could do so much, but they seemed to disappear. The Lwa were only ghosts and glimpses hiding in shadows. They were pale and sickly, unlike my strong and vital Lwa. What had happened here?

I would eventually move on to the Dominican Republic, depressed and dejected. If Vodou were not for the help and support of the people, what was it good for?

Across the border in the Dominican, I inquired about Vodou, but few understood or knew of it. The few ounfò I discovered were nearly abandoned and housed only a handful faithful. They lived in fear of the Catholic church, and political persecution. Only the most defiant would allow me into their home to talk about the old days and the belief that had been erased from this place. Those who held fast to Vodou were given my blessing. I infused them with my magic, bolstering their health and vitality. I pried the Lwa from the shadows, demanding that they do more. In the Ounfò, I begged for Bondýe to heal this sacred place, but I had never felt the presence of Bondýe, before or now. I was only aware of him through Maka and my Lwa. My dance, song and sacrifices did not bring any comfort or assistance.

I was directed to the North of the Island nation to the village of Geffarty, where a Vodou Temple was known to exist.

The long flight took me across beautiful country. The people looked into the sky with wonder that a human should be flying overhead. No news of my existence or visitation had apparently made it to the Vodou adherents of my religions homeplace, but I did not worry, for soon I would be among friends and family. Perhaps the ancestors of Maka himself.

I arrived in Geffarty and was directed to the Temple Vodou, Empereur Ernso. It was a common adobe building in the fashion of the country. It could have been a market, or an office. Only the chipped and peeling painted lettering to the right of the door recognized this as a holy place. Under the long, flat roof that served as a shade in the oppressive heat, I located a door and helped myself inside. A small, battered desk and a three-legged chair, patched with a stick lashed to the broken leg, served as a reception. Alongside was a rickety old table with hand-made souvenirs and objects of Vodou for tourists to buy. Beyond the desk was an earthen floor, uneven from years of use and neglect. Along the back wall was an alter featuring the visage of Bondýe. The image looked to be painted with fingers, dipped in hand-crushed pigments. It was rough and crude, depicting a man of ebony skin and snakes for hair, dancing. Bondýe is a word derived from the French "Bon Dieu" meaning "Good God". He is the creator of the universe and maintainer of universal order. Bondýe represents all that is good in the world. From where I was standing, in the most violent, poverty-stricken place I had ever been, it seemed as if Bondýe had abandoned his creation.

A noise behind me brought me from my thoughts. I turned to see an old man kneeling, forehead to the floor in submission. Beyond old, he was ancient, perhaps like me. As he looked up into my eyes, I see wrinkles as deep as my own. Ebony skin, and white hair that seemed to go every direction. As he stood, he was stooped in stature and his sandaled feet were flat and spread from years of walking the dirt roads and mountainous terrain of this place.

My Lwa were immediately on guard. I felt them cower and submit immediately to this person. Never had they shown submission, and I was curious, for I felt nothing.

"Byenveni, Bondýe mwen" he said with hands reverently pressed together as if in prayer (welcome, Bondýe, my god). "Mwen tande w ap vini. Se yon plezi pou mwen akeyi ou. Se yon plezi pou mwen akeyi ou. Mwen se sèvitè w papa Legba (I have heard of your coming. It is my pleasure to welcome you. I am your servant, Papa Legba)".

I was aware of a stories of papa Legba. He was an Lwa spirit that had taken on human form to connect Bondýe with the human world. Perhaps not unlike Maka and I. If this were indeed Papa Legba, he could be as old as time itself.

I kneeled on aching and rough knees before Papa Legba and bowed low. "It is my privilege to meet you Papa Legba, but I am not Bondýe, but a woman from the swamps who has come to find Bondýe and my people."

Papa Legba laughed and extended his hand to assist me to my feet. "Come, we will eat, and I will tell you why you are here".

BONDÝE

We walked a short way to a small adobe home. There was no door or windows, just openings for the slight breeze to pass, and a sturdy shelter in times of storm.

Inside was just as spartan. A small table with one chair, and a bed of palm fronds, topped with dried grass, upon which a clean white sheet was lain. Papa Legba fetched a small three-legged stool from outside and sat it opposite the chair at the table and bid me to sit.

Upon the table was a setting of dates, cold greens, and baked chicken. Two chipped pottery glasses held cool water. Papa Legba had prepared a peasant feast for us in advance of my arrival, which I gratefully accepted.

"How do you find our country to be?" He asked in strongly accented English.

"I find it to be poor, desperate and sad," said I.

"And what do you attribute this poverty and sadness to?" he asked.

"There are many gods here. Gods of the Christians, Gods of the Inca, Maya, of the Fon and the Yoruba which Maka taught me of. Today the Christian God rules this place. It strips it of its wealth. It submits it to its will. It is not a benevolent or good god, but one of greed and submission. Where are the good gods? Where has the hope and charity gone? I know only of Lwa, and the assistance they provide to me. I know not of Bondýe, who is supposed to be the creator and ruler. He is supposed to lord over all Lwa, yet my Lwa have no knowledge of him, for although they are eternal, even they have only slight memory of him. Why is not Bondýe here to save his people?"

Papa Lega thought for long moments as he picked scraps of food from between his long and brown teeth. "Bondýe is beyond the workings and lives of humanity. He is creator of all, and this small world has little attention to him, as a hill of ants to you. He must balance the universe, and this is a small piece within it. Do not dismay, for your Lwa are his creation and his servants. Your Lwa are a manifestation of Bondýe."

I was incredulous. "I know my Lwa. They are not only within me, but they are also me. They submit to no man, yet they submit to you. They have no memory of Bondýe, only a residual fear of something past. Bondýe seems to be a bad memory that we have been asked to serve, yet he does not provide protection, food, shelter of comfort for us. I have lived a long life without Bondýe, who is he to me?" At the end, I was seething with anger. All gods were false to me. All were tyrants and oppressors. Bondýe had not shown himself. Why should I follow or submit to him?

Papa Legba laughed quietly, as was his way. "All must be told", said he. "The legends and stories have been lost to time. Lost to all but me, who has kept them for these many thousands of years.

†††

The beginning is unknown, even to Bondýe. He came to conciseness in a vast void of space, where he existed and explored for an eternity. Desiring life around him, he began to seed the stars with plants, watching them grow and offering his own manipulations and desires to as they flourished.

With mischievous curiosity, Bondýe created spines, thorns, and oils to make the leaves shine in the sunlight. These were ornamental, bring pleasure to the creator.

Many eternities later, he would create creatures of all form and substance, fashioning each to his whim. All were made in harmony and peace, for Bondýe knew not hate or violence. He allowed these creatures to evolve and change over time, so that they may enjoy diversity of life. It was thought to be a paradise, but the thorns pricked and caused pain, causing the creatures to adapt. The oils burned the skin and poisoned those that ate it. Soon the creatures began to seek the flesh of others for sustenance. As eons changed, so did the life Bondýe had created. Now there was fang and claw. There was predator and prey. Bondýe saw that it had grown violent and hateful. Bondýe, was appalled at what he had made, and determined to abandon this remote world of insignificance, preferring his other creations that were more harmonious.

Bondýe created the Lwa to provide care, comfort, and support to this world in his absence. Within this offering, Lwa could only access the living world through humanity, and they must be invited through dance and song. For humanity to invite the Lwa, they must offer something in return. Something so precious that it must be of great value. It was life itself, in the form of sacrifice. Over tens of thousands of years, Lwa and humans created an uneasy alliance. That was the last we have seen of Bondýe, for he left us to fend for ourselves."

He continued, "The Lwa are exceedingly selfish and demanding. They can be both benevolent and vindictive. For these reasons, only those humans who have practiced the art of Vodou may intercede with the Lwa. This infuriated the Lwa, who wanted all men to dance, sing and worship them as Gods. For many years, the Lwa would punish any human who dare call to them. Rather than submit, humanity simply found other gods to worship. Gods that were made of lie, fabrication, and fiction. Gods that would not punish them. Gods that could be used to manipulate the masses and control all of humanity.

Bondýe became a myth. His Lwa weak and fearful. Today, only a few will offer song and dance to the Lwa. When the Lwa appear, they are ridiculed and damned. Time has all but erased the Lwa and Bondýe from civilization".

This was the story I had come to hear. I could feel my Lwa inside me, furious at the folly of their kin, and angry at the ease with which man simply erased their creator Bondýe from their lives.

Papa Legba again laughed. He sent a blanket of comfort for my Lwa, which they embraced. Papa Legba was the oldest of the Lwa. He was the leader, the center of their existence. Within this awesome visage, all Lwa felt insignificant and small. What my Lwa were learning was that Papa Legba was not all powerful and dominant at all. He was calm, and peaceful. He was not a tyrant, but a teacher. He had seen all the things that had gone wrong in the past. Rather than force them into submission, he allowed life to evolve and change.

"There is an ebb and flow to all things in the Universe. Over time, Lwa has served as servant to man, other times, man has served as servant to the Lwa. Families of great wealth become poor; families of poverty become wealthy. Health becomes illness, life becomes death. All things change over time. Many lifetimes ago I learned that the best way to embrace this world was to allow it to evolve in its own way, and in its own time. Today, I am a simple Lwa, ancient and toothless in my power. Tomorrow I may be the savior of all the world. These things are unknown. I have learned to embrace this change.

"Is there not balance?" I asked. " Can there be no place where plant, animal, human and Lwa can all exist together in harmony?"

Again, Papa Legba laughed. "I have seen many things since the beginning of time, but I have never seen harmony among all. It is simply not the way of this world."

"You speak of worlds as if there exist many. What do you know of all worlds?"

I know that Bondýe made many before this place, and that perhaps he continues today. He is easily bored, and the endless worlds in our Universe provide him with an infinite palette to work with. Somewhere, he is likely creating something new. Perhaps he has found a way to create true harmony, perhaps not. It is not for me to say."

"Is there any way for us to contact and connect with Bondýe ?" I asked.

"There was a time when he would come, but he no longer answers us. We are alone in our path."

I selected another sweet date from the plate between us. My teeth broke the skin, and I felt the sweetness fill my mouth. Such intense pleasure from such a small fruit. How could any entity possibly envision this moment? How to create flavors and taste? How to make thorns and not see that it would lead to pain? How to make roasted flesh taste so good and not know that it would become sustenance?

There was much to ponder here. I excused myself and stepped out into the bright Haitian sunlight. The heat was moist and beautiful. No breeze to ease the discomfort, but it was a familiar discomfort. One I had known all my life. I could feel the weight of my perspiration in my loose cotton gown. I could feet small stones and dirt under my feet. The mosquitos which were ever present to the uninitiated, were completely ignored to those of us who lived here.

And what of the Texas plains? The vast, wild land of dry grass and shrub. Dry winds that chapped your lips and the corners of your eyes. Dust-devils that lifted acres of dirt and strew it across the land until your entire body was dusted with it.

I thought of the cities I had traversed, with row upon row of domicile. Of ships that crossed oceans and skiffs that traversed bayou. Creatures with fin, fur, feather and skin. Everything adapted to its environment. Each unique in its ability to adapt and thrive.

I thought of the thousands of ways that the human body could endure illness, wound or trauma. Both spiritual and physical. How resilient were some, and how fragile others. Within this, I thought of my own strength and fragility. The years had made me strong of body and spirit, but I desperately wanted the comfot of another human that was not tied to their material need. I wanted to know that my gift was good, and that it brought happiness, health and comfort. Yet, I knew that as much as it was a gift, it was also a curse. There were people who coveted my gift, and if they could not embody it, they would try to control it. Like adapting fang and claw, some people adapted hard hearts, greed and a desire to dom-inate. You could not teach these people goodness, it would need to evolve over hundreds of generations, until their dis-tant relations perhaps found comfort and peace. Meanwhile, there were good people today whose lineage were destined to be the murderers, rapists and politicians of tomorrow.

This was the great puzzle. Not even our *Good God* Bondýe had been able to resolve it. He had grown tired of trying to cure something that constantly evolved into something worse. Like a cancer, all life on this world looks for the path of least resistance to obtain the best result for itself, even if it kills its host.

This was my reality. Bondýe could not cure this world. Papa Legba had tried for thousands of lifetimes and failed. All of humanity together could not create a social harmony. What chance did I have? I was a simple woman from the swamps of Louisiana. I was an outcast, a witch, a Sorciére. What could I possibly do that had not already been tried and failed? Would it be a waste of my gift to even try?

Papa Legba and I walked a long, stony lane through the countryside. It was deeply rutted from use, nearly impassable. The locals had made this road in a time past, and each dry season they came together to repair the ruts and erosion that had occurred during the rains. Every attempt to make it smooth and easily traversed was met with livestock, vehicles and people that carved divots and canyons that were easily eroded in the rainy season. No matter how many times they fixed the road, the result was always the same. Papa Legba was thinking that this was a metaphor for life. Why try to smooth the way when the next rain would just undo your effort? He did not need to say it, because I was thinking the same thing.

As we walked, I began to speak, as much to myself as to Papa Legba. "On my travels, I find good people who are ill and need healing. I provide this service so they can then provide for their children or become a valued member of their community. My small effort has a tangible and real benefit. If I feed the people of a village, they will know a moment of comfort and happiness. We dance and sing, and praise Bondýe for these gifts. Tomorrow, they may be hungry again, but in that moment, they have a life of comfort and cheer. I would offer that the man or woman that repairs this path, will benefit from a season of easier travel. They will be able to navigate with ease, if only for a few months. Their work is a gift to others who may use this path. These are moments of harmony, and therefore, they are not wasted.

I resolve that one person can make a big difference to a small part of their world. If enough people come together in this effort, it will lift a portion of humanity just a little. Perhaps this is enough?"

Papa Legba looked at the ground as he walked. His fingers entwined behind his back and whisp of his grey hair moved across his face with the rhythm of his steps. "If this is how you feel, you must act on it. This is your path. It is your vision. You must follow your heart, regardless of its benefit to the world. If you desire to use your gift in your small corner of the swamps, you are a big blessing to a small world. If you desire to use your gift for the benefit of this world, then you might only be a small blessing to a big world, but is that no less a gift?

"Let's discuss your gift," he said to me. "Tell me about how it manifests in you."

I went into detail to share what I thought were the most significant hallmarks of my magic. I made care to separate what was my own magic from that which my Lwa provided to me. Papa Legba walked impassively as he listened. He did not act or react to my magic, as if every Manbo and ever Lwa could achieve these things, even though we both knew I alone had these gifts.

Ahead was a small farm, and we stopped for a light meal of boiled eggs and goat's milk. Papa Legba blessed the home and our host, who bowed low and returned to the toil of her day. " This is how I share my gift today. I ask little, share my blessings, and my magic to make their lives easier. It keeps the embers of Bondýe alive, if only the smallest spark."

"Could you do more?" I asked. "Is this all you have to offer?"

"As I said earlier, my participation can be significant or minor, depending on the needs of the world. In this moment, this is what my small world needs. A big magic to a small place."

"And what would be required of the world for you to be a small magic in a big world," asked I.

"Just ask, "was all he said.

†††

Papa Legba came to me in the dark of night. I had been using my magic to harvest logs and branches from the area surrounding the temple and piling them up. Smiling, he raised his arms, beckoned to all Lwa to come to us. My Lwa were first to come, they towered over our heads, reveling in this preparation. They called to the others, who were hiding in the forest and trembling with fear. Slowly, they came. With rarely heard laughter, I raised my arms high and logs from distant places in the forest came flying in. Whole trees, root and all, until the pile was as high as the temple. Papa Legba lit the pyre and beckoned the Lwa to us with dance and song. I joined in and together we resurrected a long-dead celebration of Bondýe .

With a calming smile, the physical appearance of Papa Legba dissolved into spirit, rising beyond the flames a hundred meters into the sky and reflecting the firelight in all directions. His outspread arms seemed to hold all of humanity. I called to Maka, to my parents, to Ten, bidding them to join us, and from the fire all came.

Papa Legba extended an arm down to me, and I took his hand, and felt my own physical body dissolve into spirit and I became something ethereal. My spirit body rose, towering even over Papa Legba. I looked down on all of Santa Domingo and Haiti. With tears flowing down my sprit face, I opened my arms to the world, spreading a goodness that was palpable around the globe.

Papa Legba and I were lost in our dance and song. It seemed as if a hundred Lwa were with us, and more appearing from every direction as the fire raged. So lost was I, that I did not recognize Papa Legba had reverted to his human form, kneeling, forehead to the ground in submission. One by one, each Lwa bowed low until only myself and my small family were left dancing, oblivious to the world around us.

It was the stillness of the night that caught my attention. No night sounds but my breathing and the crackle of the fire. I became aware of my four Lwa bristling with ferocity while those around us cowered in submission. My Lwa, Maka and my parents surrounded me as a barrier against ancient magic.

I turned to face Bondýe . He was black as coal with thick stems of hair falling about his head and face. He was bare of chest except for the strings of feathers, tin and bone around his neck. He wore a brilliant indigo wrap around his waist and his bare feet were covered in the island dust. Bondýe had come home.

Slowly I raised my hands, palms out, my eyes looking directly into his. I gently pumped my arms. I slowly gyrated my hips. I opened my mouth and a primal howl came out, long and loud. My feet began to stomp the ground, bringing up small clouds of dust. My movements quickened and my howl became a low, mournful chant. My Lwa and family never showed respect to the Good God, they gathered around me protectively and absorbed my dance and song as if to keep it from Bondýe .

My dance was not for Bondýe , but for myself. I was angry that this almighty creator of all things would abandon all, leaving us to the wanderings of evolution. I was showing him an example of how one small person in one small village could make a real difference. I wanted to show him that he gave up too early. That this world was worth more than he had given it.

Bondýe bowed his head slightly as an admission. He then evaporated, leaving nothing of his presence but the impressions of feet where he had stood. A moment of absolute quiet, then all rose to their feet and turned to me. Still as stone they stood until Papa Legba bowed low before me, inspiring all others present to do the same. In that moment, my Lwa knelt in submission to me while Maka, Ten and my parents stood looking on with hope and respect.

Bondýe had left this world, but this time he had left an emissary to guide and support this world. He wove into my spirit a greater magic, and the compassion to control it. He amplified my judgement, for it would be essential in the centuries to come. He left me with a sense of purpose and peace, and I welcomed it.

The humble witch of the swamp was now the savior of all.

The End.

DRAWINGS AND NOTES